The Other Malcolm—
"Shorty" Jarvis

The Other Malcolm—"Shorty" Jarvis
His Memoir

by MALCOLM "SHORTY" JARVIS
with PAUL D. NICHOLS

Edited by CORNEL R. WEST

McFarland & Company, Inc., Publishers
Jefferson, North Carolina, and London

Publisher's note: Shorty Jarvis died on September 15, 1998, shortly after the manuscript for this book was essentially completed.

Frontispiece and front cover: Malcolm "Shorty" Jarvis

The present work is a reprint of the illustrated case bound edition of The Other Malcolm—"Shorty" Jarvis: His Memoir, *first published in 2001 by McFarland.*

LIBRARY OF CONGRESS CATALOGUING-IN-PUBLICATION DATA

Jarvis, Malcolm, d. 1998.
    The other Malcolm—"Shorty" Jarvis : his memoir / by Malcolm "Shorty" Jarvis, with Paul D. Nichols ; edited by Cornel R. West.
       p.   cm.
    Includes index.

    ISBN 978-0-7864-4057-3
    softcover : 50# alkaline paper ∞

    1. Jarvis, Malcolm, d. 1998. 2. X, Malcolm, 1925–1965—Friends and associates. 3. Black Muslims—Biography. 4. Jazz musicians—United States—Biography. 5. African Americans—Biography.
I. Nichols, Paul D., 1952– . II. West, Cornel. III. Title.
BP223.Z8J374   2008
973.9'092—dc21
[B]
                                                      2001030086

British Library cataloguing data are available

©The estate of Malcolm Louis Jarvis, Sr., and Paul D. Nichols. All rights reserved

No part of this book may be reproduced or transmitted in any form or by any means, electronic or mechanical, including photocopying or recording, or by any information storage and retrieval system, without permission in writing from the publisher.

Manufactured in the United States of America

McFarland & Company, Inc., Publishers
  Box 611, Jefferson, North Carolina 28640
    www.mcfarlandpub.com

In memory of both
Malcolm L. Jarvis
and Malcolm X
—*P.D.N.*

Acknowledgments I
by Malcolm "Shorty" Jarvis

> Learn to put hope in your brains, instead of dope in your veins.
> Evil is injected from without to within.
> Goodness originates in the heart.
> —*Malcolm "Shorty" Jarvis*

It has been a privilege, an honor and my greatest pleasure to have known and to have associated with some of the world's greatest jazz musicians, many of whom originated in Boston, Massachusetts. Regretfully, some are not with us today; however, the world has been left with wonderful memories and original styles of playing music which will never be forgotten. With pride, I'm very happy to announce that the vast majority of those musicians with whom I grew up have gone on to become world famous. Of course, there were others who never made it to the top due to unforeseen circumstances in their private lives.

A list such as this one can only represent my best attempts at trying to recall and to honor all those who have inspired me, musically. Unfortunately, such a list can never be complete. I ask humbly the forgiveness of those whom I have omitted. My grateful acknowledgments go to the following who were all members of the American Federation of Musicians, Local 535, which was located at 409 Mass Avenue, Boston, Massachusetts (Local 535 has since merged with Local 9, to become Local 9-535): Billy Arnold (drums), Irving Ashby (guitar), Wayne Boyd (guitar), Paul Broadnax (piano), Paul Brown (bass, cello and violin), Eddie Buster (piano), Robert Buster (piano, organ and bass), Eugene

Caines (trumpet), Tasker Crossen (bass), Allen Dawson (drums), Highland Diggs (piano), Roy Eldridge (trumpet), Harold "Fordy" Ford, Jr. (drums), Marcus Foster (drums), Ricky Gale (bass), Joe Gordon (trumpet), William Grant (drums), Roy Haynes (drums), Harold Holt (alto saxophone), Clifford O. Jarvis, Sr. (trumpet), Francis Johnson (guitar), Hopeton Johnson (piano), Lennie Johnson (trumpet), Sonny Jones (drums), Harold Layne (drums), Herby Lee, Sr. (alto saxophone, M.C. & dancer), Roland Lee (bass), Willis Lee (E-flat baritone saxophone), Sebastian Lewis (piano), Lou Lima (tenor saxophone), Edward Logan (bass), Richard Lowery, Jr. (trumpet), Andrew "Andy" McGhee (tenor saxophone), Maceo O'Brien (trumpet), Ralph Peace (trumpet), George Pearson (piano and organ), William Pearson (alto saxophone), Bazeley Perry (drums), Joseph Perry (baritone and tenor saxophones), Raymond Perry (alto saxophone and violin), Walter Radcliffe (piano), Joseph Riddick (drums), Rudolph Riley (piano), Sam Rivers (tenor saxophone), Hillary Rose (organ), Preston Saniford (piano), Gladstone Scott (tenor saxophone), Tommy Simmons (piano and vocalist), Mable Simms (piano), Emery Smith (piano), Jay Talbot (tenor saxophone), Clark Terry (trumpet), Ernest Trotman (piano), Lloyd Trotman (bass), Stanley Trotman (piano), James Tyler (alto and tenor saxophones), Judson Watts (baritone, alto and tenor saxophones), Lou West (alto saxophone), T.J. Wheeler (guitar, vocalist), Floyd Williams (drums), Frederick Williams (tenor saxophone), Tillman Williams (alto and tenor saxophones), Linwood Wilson (guitar).

These were my personal friends, musical friends and fraternal brothers and sisters. My affiliation with great and wonderfully creative people has afforded me a formal education for which I am eternally grateful.

Acknowledgments II
by Paul D. Nichols

This project was one which consumed me for two years before my recent marriage. I had to call on the services of a number of friends and family, and all were most supportive. Below, I would like to list just a few of these people:

First, I thank Pastor Virgil Wood for making the introduction. If he had not introduced me to Shorty, I would not have been offered this wonderful opportunity. I would also like to thank John Shields, Theresa Donovan and the staff and students at the Dearborn Middle School, in Boston, for welcoming Shorty to such an extent that Shorty felt comfortable enough to carry on a four hour conversation with me after his appearance, laying the groundwork for our negotiating the production of this book. I would also like to thank Dr. Ray Peterson, Joanie Pierce and the staff and students at Hyde Park High School, for it was here that Shorty made his very last, live public presentation.

I would like to thank my family members (my parents, Joseph and Stella Nichols, in particular) for putting up with my overall absence as I was literally shut off in Connecticut many weekends and nearly two full summers. I would like to thank Amy Bitcover and Paula Herndon for their editing and brainstorming ideas for the original concept of the book, and Paula for visiting with Shorty during the initial stages of our negotiations. I'd like to thank Merry Foxworth for her dutiful word processing of the initial publisher listings. It was from these listings that we eventually found McFarland & Company. I would like to thank my friends, Matthew Atobe, Mansur, Dr. Sang Won Park, N 'Gadi Jean-Pierre, Brian Porter and Dr. Edward Williams for putting up with many readings and preliminary edits of the original manuscript.

As concerns all those teachers in all the schools to which I had taken the project, I can't thank you enough for reading, rereading, and listening to preliminary drafts of many of these pages—or for simply encouraging me: Rosalind Agwu-Igbani, Michael Allen, John Barnes, Trudy Brennan, Comanceda Brown, Patricia Brown, Carey Dardompré, Irene Fontanez, Ian Glaude, Kathy Guerin, Damon Halback, Sensei John Irving, Sylvia Johnson, Kim Kamborian, Virginia Kemp, Patrick Lamerson, Francine Lockhart, Bill Owens, Cruz Sanabria, Sarah Teasdale, Hassan Williams, Tanya Wisdom—just to name a few.

I would like to thank Joel Davidson and the Davidson family for both their legal support and their encouragement. Thanks also to my neighbor Michelle Ross for her encouragement and her introduction to Ferdinand Jones (the eminent jazz psychologist then serving as a professor emeritus at Brown University) who was the first person to read the first rough draft of the entire manuscript. His finding it "fascinating" gave me a "second wind." I thank him for his timely comments, his efforts and suggestions. I'd like to thank Shorty's friends and family including his wife, "Lady Liz" Jarvis, his childhood buddy, Joe Reddick, his son "Butchy," and the many of his musician friends I've met while working on this project.

My most heartfelt thanks go to my longtime friend and spiritual brother, Cornel R. West, for the editing, the wonderful introduction, the listening, just the "being there" throughout the entire project. Finally, this project could not have been made possible without both the support and assistance of my wife, Pamela. Her dedicated and fastidious formatting of the manuscript, and her countless hours of proofreading were nearly as important as the actual writing of the book.

Lastly, to all of those whose assistance I have lapsed in recalling, my most humble apologies and my deepest gratitude. This project truly was a labor of love.

Contents

Acknowledgments I by Malcolm "Shorty" Jarvis — vii
Acknowledgments II by Paul D. Nichols — ix
Preface by Paul D. Nichols — 1
Introduction by Cornel R. West — 5

1	Light of Truth	7
2	The Family	14
3	Reminiscing	24
4	Trial and Incarceration	60
5	Transgression—of the Mind	74
6	The Black Man and Christianity	106
7	Pivotal Events	124
8	The Vision	138
9	Extraordinary Phenomena	143
10	Dreams	150

Afterword by Paul D. Nichols — 154
Index — 163

IN HONOR OF BLACK WOMEN

Black women ... Our African queens, know intrinsically...
They are the Mother of us all...
Mankind itself sprang forth from her loins...
Star that she is...
In the Garden of Eden ... even God ... Himself
Chose to put Adam to sleep...
In order that He might create and commune with her...
To establish a Divine Intimacy with her...
Borne of Heaven ... I am sure
He had a lot to say—information which he has
Stored in every cell of her Heavenly Body...
(In truth, she is so desirable.... It is no wonder that
In class-conscious Brazil, for example, inter-racial
Marriage is encouraged ... and in the USA ... with the passing
Years...I've seen more and more of our women involved in
Inter-racial relationships—even on TV...
That it's 'Playing in Peoria' ... is yet a further
Testimony ... Nay ... A Living 'Ode' ... to the beauty of our women...)
It is time to behold and to uphold our women ... anew—
And time for our women to once again behold and
Honor themselves...

—by Malcolm "Shorty" Jarvis

Preface
by Paul D. Nichols

He was an Everyman, successful in his larger responsibilities: a dutiful husband; a father, successfully raising two children; a retired employee; a black man, surviving in America for 75 years—after a rough start in life. At that time in his life, he had been in touch with one who would be considered great: Malcolm X.

Like Malcolm X, Shorty, too, was uncommon: for a man, completing a formal education spanning nine grades only, he was uncommonly bright—and well-spoken; he had an unquenchable thirst for knowledge—until his dying day; ultimately, he was a thinker and a wise man. Yet, for his association with Malcolm X, he would at once be lauded and lambasted. For the first time, we have been afforded a closer glimpse at that relationship (and much more) as told by Shorty himself. (In this book, Shorty also shares poetic thoughts about life in a refreshing and uncommon way. In a word, he develops his book by delving ever deeper into his own thoughts and reflections on his life.)

It is apparent, Shorty was—as he would always say about others—a "highly spiritually-endowed man." But Shorty felt that all the others who had written about him had missed the mark, relative to his importance in the formative years of Malcolm X's spiritual development. On the contrary, in their discussions of Shorty, these other writers spent their time dabbling in caricature.

The Other Malcolm— "Shorty" Jarvis, is the story of Malcolm X's best friend (prior to Malcolm X's conversion to Islam) and "running buddy," Malcolm "Shorty" Jarvis. Ultimately, Mr. Jarvis has written this book to set the record straight. He feels he has been caricatured both by Alex Haley in *The Autobiography of Malcolm X* and by Spike Lee—who played the part of "Shorty" in his movie *Malcolm X*. In fact, by his own account, Shorty thought both portrayed him as an otiose "buffoon."

To that end, this book challenges the misconceptions about Shorty now existing in the media. For example, according to Alex Haley, Malcolm X himself said Shorty was his Svengali—for the negative in his life. Accounts like these are simply not true. First of all, I think both Malcolms shared that title role. But, more importantly, it was Shorty, grounded by his deep spiritual background, who inspired a spiritual change in Malcolm Little—who also had a strong religious background. And in this regard, I agree, Shorty was Malcolm Little's Svengali. (In fact, what is most exciting about this book is that for the first time, the process, the mechanism whereby both Shorty and Malcolm X were transformed from hardened street hustlers to reformed men, is shared by Shorty with his readers.)

As this book clarifies some issues—namely his age, his musical interests, his family background, and the origins and the nature of his relationship with the then Malcolm Little—I trust, in reading his story, you will come to see that to the best of his knowledge, it was Shorty who was the first to introduce Malcolm X to Islam. It was because of Shorty's relationship and resultant experiences with Abdul Hameed that the Imam paid them prison visits—further initiating Malcolm X in the way of things spiritual. It was Shorty who encouraged Malcolm X and the Thaxton Brothers to engage in non-Western spiritual practices and beliefs while they were in prison. And while incarcerated, it was Shorty who, with his life, demonstrated to Malcolm X the degree to which he too could transform himself. By learning to play music well enough to write a beautiful concerto, Shorty's spiritual development and grounding inspired Malcolm X's spiritual search, culminating in his spiritual transformation.

In other words, were it not for Shorty, in that space and time, there would not have been a Malcolm X, as the world came to know him. Shorty became the channel through which Malcolm X gained inspiration to investigate his own spiritual dimensions—a conduit through which Malcolm X received his spiritual insights. Shorty was far from a "buffoon."

Malcolm "Shorty" Jarvis with his horn. In his prime, his playing resembled a cross between the sounds of Roy Eldridge and Dizzy Gillespie.

In sum, I think, since the writing of *The Autobiography*, all of us wanted to know, "Who was Shorty, really?" Well, for the first time in print, Shorty has given all of us the opportunity to find out.

Introduction
by Cornel R. West

Malcolm "Shorty" Jarvis is known to the world as the "other" Malcolm—the friend of Malcolm X. Yet he is a fascinating and formidable figure in his own right. His story is now available to us owing to the tremendous discipline and determination of my friend and Harvard classmate, Paul Nichols. Shorty's moving sojourn is rooted in the rich spirituality of red and black people in America that flows from Indian ritual to Christian church to Islamic mosque.

As Paul Nichols rightly stresses, Shorty's life was grounded in black music. His trumpet, his compositions, and his listening to the great jazz musicians constituted a major source of sustenance in his life. In fact, when I first met Shorty in my office with Paul, he struck me as one of the most musical persons I had ever encountered. His walk, his talk, his linguistic intonations and inflections all had the timing of a life-musician who had mastered the art and craft of living. We had planned to meet and talk for an hour or so; we stayed together over four consecutive hours.

Shorty's story is not only a heartfelt narrative of a self-loving and self-respecting black man in the belly of a beast called twentieth century America. It is also a necessary correction to the numerous errors—and sometimes lies—about Shorty as rendered in the great classic, *The Autobiography of Malcolm X,* by the late Alex Haley.

Shorty was quite upset about the mendacious characterizations of himself in books and films on Malcolm X. He harbored no bitterness or hatred toward the authors of these works; he simply wanted to set the record straight.

Now he, with the indefatigable work of Paul Nichols, has told his story in his words to the world, and his wisdom, maturity, love—and painful struggle—shine through!

1
Light of Truth

Truth (often a threat to unnatural power, and a fuel to natural power) is the acquisition of honesty, knowledge and integrity. A wise man interested in self-improvement who is inspired by his own soul, will cut off the head of the serpent, ego, with the sword of knowledge.

Justice, on the other hand, appears as a blindfolded female holding a set of scales slightly off-balance. This display can be seen on most government, state and municipal buildings. It clearly depicts justice as being blind. I'm surprised there isn't a blindfold on the Statue of Liberty.

People should be judged by their deeds, qualifications and actions, not the color of their skin. Affirmative Action and Civil Rights have all but been shot down by the federal government. "Equal Opportunity" has proven also to be a big joke to minority people. There is no such a thing as freedom, justice and equality for all.

The poverty level has grown tremendously. People who want work are unemployed. People who think their jobs have made them free are enslaved by their own sense of freedom, for even nature herself isn't free from the daily ravages brought upon her by mankind.

Abraham Lincoln once said, "You can fool some of the people some of the time; but, you can't fool all of the people all of the time." Racial prejudice should be made an international crime.

—*by Malcolm "Shorty" Jarvis*

    At this point, I trust you have observed the light of truth concerning several misconceptions perpetuated in the media about me: I play trumpet, not saxophone; I was never ten years older than Malcolm

X; neither my mother nor any other part of my family lived in any part of Michigan at that time—or ever; playing pool was the only work I did in a pool hall; I was not into drugs—although I was a street tough, I was both a classy and a classic type of guy (Why else would Malcolm X and I associate with each other? We were birds of a feather); I was not a draft dodger—I never took glycerin or any other drugs to affect the functioning of my heart in order to avoid the draft; I never conked Malcolm X's hair (He always had his hair done at Fogey's barber shop. Fogey died a few years ago—otherwise, he'd have told you himself); I never dated any of the white girls in our "gang"—hence the "Ode to Black Women"; the list goes on. Suffice to say, I feel the media have portrayed me unfairly. Yet, these facts do not in any way alter the overriding message of that venerable book, *The Autobiography of Malcolm X*. In this chapter, I would like to, without malice, simply set the record straight and to reflect on several issues of personal importance.

Page 182, The Autobiography of Malcolm X

Malcolm admits to the fact that his baptism into public speaking was made through his taking part in the Norfolk Prison Colony's weekly debating program. Both Malcolm and I looked forward to these debates. While Malcolm was clearly the speaker at these sessions, I served by keeping him on track and by providing strategically poignant facts whenever I sensed he needed some help.

Page 191

It says, "Later, I found out in prison, Shorty had studied musical composition. He even progressed to writing some pieces; one of them he named, 'The Bastille Concerto.'" This remark was partly true. I did write a composition and named it, "The Bastille Concerto." The light of truth is, I studied harmony, theory and composition from the Boston University Extension school. Malcolm was aware of this, because he lodged just across the hall in the same domicile at the Norfolk Prison Colony. While composing the concerto, I showed him my sketches in the process. Somebody misunderstood that quote for his book when he made it.

Page 197 (bottom of page)

Malcolm comments, "Allah blessed me to remain true, firm and strong in my faith in Islam, despite the many severe trials of my faith. When events produced a crisis between Mr. Muhammad and me, I told him from the beginning, with all the sincerity I had in me, I believed in him more strongly than he believed in himself." With all due respect to Mr. Muhammad, these were very heavy words spoken to him by one whom he taught wisdom and knowledge. That Mr. Muhammad—like any good father—would not do what it took (even if that meant changing his behavior) to keep a dutiful son under the wings of his protection and akin with the overall goals and mission of the family was simply both a shame and a disservice to all who Malcolm X served in The Nation.

Page 198

Malcolm said, "Because of envy and jealousy, Mr. Muhammad and I are not together. I had more faith in him than I could ever have in any other man upon the face of the earth."

"What goes around, comes around"—with no respect for persons. The tragedy within the tragedy here is that later the self-same indiscretion for which Malcolm X's brother was ejected from The Nation was the self-same infraction which was threatening to destroy The Nation from the inside out.

Page 189 (first paragraph)

Malcolm says, "The teacher himself was later accused as an immoral person." The world will never know the extent to which this fact devastated Malcolm X.

Page 187 (bottom of page)

He plainly made it clear how Allah would protect His Messenger against any opposition; but, only as long as the Messenger himself didn't deviate from the light of truth.

Page 188 (top of page)

Malcolm says, "We were taught that Allah would cause turmoil in the minds of defectors." This is what Malcolm thought happened to his brother Reginald. He felt Reginald had brought the curse of his mentors down upon himself. He was sick at heart from within to know, to see and to feel a taste of the wrath of the Supreme Power exacted upon a loved member of his own family. But at the time, the roots of Malcolm's allegiance to Elijah Muhammad ran deeper than those toward his own blood.

Page 187

He says, "I knew Mr. Muhammad was right, and my brother wrong. Little did I realize then, the day would come when Mr. Muhammad would be accused by his own sons as being guilty of the same immoral acts for which he judged Reginald and so many others."

As a staunch believer in the Supreme Power, I understand and appreciate Malcolm's deep respect for the chastisement of Allah, of those who go astray. This applies to those who have seen the light of truth and know better. Yet, he felt Reginald, being his blood brother, and being new to the religion, should have been given special forgiveness, reconsideration and reinstatement into the Nation of Islam. This was not the case in the eyes of Mr. Muhammad. Malcolm failed to see what I saw at that time. Mr. Muhammad was not in a position to forgive Reginald. If he had forgiven Reginald, it would have jeopardized his position as the Messenger, causing repercussions, and later the Nation would have experienced serious problems—ironically, that happened anyway.

Evidently, Reginald was not worth the risk to Mr. Muhammad. The stakes were much too high. This decision was made by Mr. Muhammad with no regard as to what was going on in his personal life—and would later be revealed.

The judgment of Mr. Muhammad was not for any mortal human being to make. It was the responsibility of the Supreme Power of Allah. Not understanding the application of this spiritual truth, Malcolm carried a personal grudge in his heart that would later lead to complications. What had occurred was that blood, being thicker than water, caused a serious misunderstanding between Malcolm and Mr. Muhammad. The immoral accusations of Mr. Muhammad revealed to Malcolm a wise proverb which he learned from his theological studies: "Judge not, lest ye be judged." To add injury to insult, later, Reginald would be considered mentally incompetent.

Page 199 (bottom)

Malcolm says, in reference to Mr. Muhammad, "I worshipped him." Malcolm held devoted love in his heart for Mr. Elijah Muhammad, regardless of the circumstances which developed later. Malcolm's love was similar to the undying love the world has held for Jesus Christ over two thousand years and continues, through Christianity, to claim hold of to this day—despite both the trumped-up charges brought against Him, and the later slaughters, heresies and abuses many have made in the name of Christianity. In fact, the same world which crucified Him, claims to believe in and preach about His teachings. It seems the case of Malcolm and Mr. Muhammad is a case of history repeating itself.

Page 208

Malcolm was talking about his listening to Mr. Muhammad. He explained how he listened intently to his teacher, Mr. W.D. Fard. Mr. Muhammad said he (Malcolm) listened with an open heart and mind. He never doubted anything his Savior taught. For a person to learn anything, they must listen to learn and concentrate to remember it. When a student being taught displays doubt to the teacher, the teacher's natural inclination is to think he is wasting his time trying to get through to a doubting Thomas with a negative attitude. Malcolm was full of devotion and profound love for Mr. Muhammad and his teachings. Unfortunately, in the final analysis, his faith was unfounded.

Page 226

Malcolm said, "While a man must at all times respect his woman, he needs at the same time to understand and to control her if he expects to get any respect. I didn't consider it possible for me to love any woman. I had too much experience. The women I knew were tricky, deceitful and all but untrustworthy flesh." To the best of my recollection, in his life, the only women who earned Malcolm's total respect were the women of his family and Ms. Gloria Strother. She was the character named Laura in the Spike Lee movie *Malcolm X*.

I don't make the claim that I knew Malcolm completely. I feel simply that I knew him better than most other people. Yet, one thing about him continues to perplex me. Even at this time, I still find myself wondering why Malcolm didn't marry according to the Moslem tradition. He informed Mr. Muhammad of his matrimonial intentions. As an Imam (Moslem minister), Mr. Muhammad had that authority. In 1958, he and Mr. Muhammad were on the best of terms. That was the year of his marriage. Also, with Malcolm having publicly expressed his feelings about the white race of people, I don't understand why Mr. Muhammad permitted Malcolm's marriage to be performed by a white justice of the peace.

In his *Autobiography*, he referred to this Justice of the Peace as, "An old hunchbacked white man." My question is, why didn't Mr. Muhammad perform the ceremony? I wish I knew the answer. That will have to come from his wife's memoirs—God rest her soul—or his children. It's doubtful the world will ever know the answer. In all probability, his family might feel many things in Malcolm X's life should be kept private, as they are none of anybody's business. But, his being a world-renowned public figure, the world has a right to know the whole truth. For the younger generation, which is both taught and influenced by some of Malcolm's teachings, that information deserves to have been made right, shed by the light of truth.

Page 237

Malcolm also said, "Through the white man's powerful communication media, our brainwashed brothers and sisters (and the devils too) across the United States were going to see, hear and read Mr. Muhammad's teachings, which cut back and forth like a two edged sword." That remark showed deep respect, dedication, devotion, and insight.

Page 237 (middle of the page)

Malcolm's idea of a black newspaper for the Moslems started when he wrote a weekly column for the *Amsterdam News*, a New York City-based, black newspaper. He said, "Mr. Muhammad agreed to write a column for the *Amsterdam News*, as well. His news space was transferred to another black newspaper, *The Los Angeles Dispatch*." Malcolm now had the news media working from the East Coast, and the West Coast. Both ends were working towards the home base of Chicago, in the middle.

This brilliant strategy has never been equaled. Malcolm said, "I kept wanting to start our own newspaper that would be filled with news from the Nation of Islam." Malcolm worked at the Los Angeles office long enough to observe how a newspaper was put together. Once he saw something done, he knew how to do it himself. One day a month he said, "I'd lock up in a room and assemble my material and pictures for a printer I knew. I named the newspaper, *Muhammad Speaks*." He locked up once a month in order to accomplish his task, which successfully demonstrates his respect for our venerable practice of isolation (see Chapter 5, "Transgression of the Mind") which, apparently, he continued after prison.

Page 238

He said he founded the newspaper *Muhammad Speaks*. He claimed the responsibility for the naming of it.

Why at this late date, I wonder, have I never heard anyone credit Malcolm X for this fact? To the best of my knowledge, no mention has ever surfaced about this feat, one of Malcolm X's more lasting accomplishments. It's very strange. His founding of the newspaper should be common knowledge. If it is, it has been kept relatively quiet. (In recent years, the paper's name has been changed to, *The Final Call*.)

Page 287 (top of page)

Malcolm's own words, "I believed so strongly in Mr. Muhammad that I would have hurled myself between him and an assassin." I believe these words speak for themselves.

2
The Family

Life is a game
Put your heart into it
Life is a game
Act your part in it
Life is a joke
Make a jest of it
Life is a job
Make the best of it
Life is a song
In either key—
Major or minor—
Which shall it be?
The choice is yours.

—Adapted by Malcolm "Shorty" Jarvis

THE FAMILY PRAYER ACKNOWLEDGMENT

All praise is due Allah
Who is All and All...
Who is ... Everything Contained Within Everything ... who is ... 360 degrees of spiritual and physical knowledge.
Who is ... an ordered system of ideas that are harmonious and self-inclusive...

Who is ... the creator of imagination ... who is ... the giver of the transgression of the mind theory...
Master of myself, within myself...
All praise is due the Supreme Power, "Allah."

2. The Family

During the year of the Supreme Power, September 11, 1923, I, Malcolm L. Jarvis (later known as "Shorty"), was born in the Roxbury section of Boston, Massachusetts. My mother's maiden name was Ethel Frances White. My father's name was Clifford Osbourn Jarvis. My grandmother's maternal name was Lucy Ann Spratley. In tracing my family tree, I estimate the date of my grandmother's birth to have been the year of 1864, in Newport News, Virginia; the day, October tenth. On many occasions when I was a young man, Grandmother told me a great deal about the family history. Her vivid memory of her childhood and parents amazed me. She told me her grandparents were slaves during the British and American war of 1812. (That was 52 years before her birth.) When she was a young lady, her parents related this family history (and more) to her that she might do the same for future generations. Grandmother also told me that her grandparents were Iroquois Indians and slaves for white people. By taking a "second look" at her, one could easily see the Indian in her reddish, light-brown complexion, and straight black hair. This being true, then a good part of the family tree on Grandmother's side belongs to the Iroquoian-Caddoan stock of the North American Indians. My research shows the Iroquois Indians were comprised of six nations: Seneca, Cayuga, Oneida, Onondaga Mohawk, and Tuscarora.

Over the years I have realized, I must have received, by heredity, some of the Indian spiritual qualities—and some were inculcated by my grandparents. Of all the grandchildren in the family, I was Grandmother's favorite. She spent countless hours telling me of intricate things pertaining to the proclivities of life itself. One time I became sick, Grandmother, taking over from my mother, administered some of her Indian remedies. They were mostly composed of the herbs of the earth; usually, something like: sassafras tea, oil of eucalyptus, harlequin oil and many more I can't think of at the moment. For sure, her remedies were very effective.

October tenth, 1964, one month after my forty-first birthday, I remember grandmother received a certificate of congratulations from the late president, Dwight D. Eisenhower, for reaching her 100th birthday. In celebration of her achievement, the family had a reunion party that went on for three days and nights. Five generations of family members attended. Great and great-great grandchildren were present. I thought it so fantastic, her being the progenitor of all these beautiful people, all telling family stories and just enjoying each other's company. It was just beautiful.

For some strange reason, all my life, I have been very inquisitive about my family's history and also about people who were close friends of the family. If what I have been told is the truth—and I do believe it is—then I can readily understand the depth of spirituality that has existed in my family for over two hundred years.

I feel so sad when I remember Grandmother's passing in October 1966, just a few days short of her 102nd birthday. Funeral services were held at the Union Baptist Church, 874 Main Street, Cambridge, Massachusetts. This church has been our family church home for more than 75 years, and stands in very good condition to this day. Grandmother's interment was at the Mount Hope Cemetery in Mattapan, Massachusetts. Almost every year since her departure from us, I have visited her gravesite in remembrance, and have said a prayer or two. Atmospherically and spiritually, her presence is still felt and will never be forgotten by the family and me.

Peter Miles White was the beloved husband of Lucy Ann Spratley and my grandfather. Likewise, he was born in Newport News, Virginia, March 4, 1862. Grandfather was about five feet seven inches tall, jet black in complexion with a gentle smile and a soft-spoken voice. He passed away on July 18, 1937, at age 75. At the time, I was 14 years old. I recall, Grandmother would not permit his body to lie in the funeral parlor. She had the undertaker bring him home for the family and friends to view. That was a practice seldom heard of at the time—to have the deceased lie "in state," at home.

Grandfather also spent a lot of time with me when I was a little boy. I like to remember and to think of him in the same way as the Bible referred to both Jesus and His disciples, "fishers of men." In speaking to me, he was always busy planting his mental seeds of life in my young, fertile mind. This habit he performed on other people also. He was wise enough to know, in time, his mental seeds would bear within me the fruit of spirituality and faith in the Supreme Power. Of all the stories he told me, my favorite was the one about the racehorse and his jockey. It went something like this:

One day, while we were just out strolling, Grandfather said to me, "Son, let me tell you a story I hope you will remember as long as you live. One day at the racetrack a horse trainer accused a jockey of losing a race deliberately.

"The jockey proclaimed, 'The horse was lazy and didn't care to win.'

"The trainer answered, 'If you had but taken a little time to pet the horse before the race and show him some loving care, you could have changed all that. The horse needed some kindness and encouragement, not to be beaten with a whip.' The moral of the story is, a 'don't care' horse will always lose the race or throw his jockey off his back."

Grandfather was a member of the Masonic organization called "The Odd Fellows." He was also a deacon and one of the oldest members of the Union Baptist Church. The church was founded in the year 1878, on October 27, and [in 1998 was] 120 years old. Its history is renowned. The late Dr. Martin Luther King, Jr., used to preach from the pulpit of this church. At that time, he was studying for his Ph.D. degree at Boston University. In past years, the church has served as an historical way station for weary travelers whose souls had thirst and hungered for nourishment, enlightenment, righteousness and spirituality. May the soul of Grandfather rest in peace—all the while, it is still alive in me.

Peter and Lucy White had ten children: two boys and eight girls. The boys were named after Grandfather: Peter and Miles. Both passed on very early in life.

Lou Virginia White, the first daughter, was better known to the family as Aunt Jennie. She always seemed to know that the way to a child's heart was through the stomach. How I remember all those pies and cakes she used to bake, and I always tried to catch them coming hot out of the oven. I used to make it my business to visit her every Sunday morning before going to church. Etta and Edna White, daughters number two and three, passed on very early in life. Aunt Jennie married Louis Morrison and gave him a son named Louis Morrison, Jr. During his life, Louis Jr. married twice. His first wife was named Dorothy Bonito, and she gave him four children: two boys and two girls. They were Peter, Phillip, Margie and J. Clair. Dorothy passed on, and Louis Jr. later married a second time. Wife number two was a Caucasian and of British and Irish descent. Her name was Barbara Irish. She was originally from the state of Maine. Her family tree shows her ancestors were Brewsters who came to this country on the good ship *Mayflower* (the self-same which brought the Pilgrims from England to Plymouth, Massachusetts, landing upon the famous Plymouth Rock—about which Malcolm X once spoke).

Barbara gave Louis Jr. five children. They were: Virginia, David, Carol, Connie and Sharon. Louis Junior's total number of children was

Phil Morrison, Howard McGee and Walter Radcliffe.

nine. Most of them are married and have families of their own. In fact, overall, my family has grown so, I find it very hard to keep up with its growth.

As concerns the offspring of Louis Junior's first wife, I am proud to announce that my cousin Phillip Morrison has established himself as a prominent musician, poet and composer. He resides presently in Atlanta, Georgia.

Ethel Frances White, daughter number four, was my mother. My father's name was Clifford Osbourn Jarvis. Ethel gave Clifford five children: Herbert, sister Elsie, brother Clifford, Donald and myself (Malcolm). I recall as a young boy, Herbert was in and out of prison. He would spend two or three years in prison, get released, and within a few months would break the law and find himself back in prison. That was the way most of his life went. He passed on at age 56. Elsie, my one and only sister, was a lovable, kindhearted person with a charming personality. She married Bruds Hodges of Roxbury. She departed this life in 1949. At that time, I had served three and one half years in Norfolk Prison Colony with the late Malcolm X. I was permitted to go to her funeral in handcuffs and returned to prison. The experience of seeing my sister lying at rest and being returned to prison left a vivid impression on my mind. I felt I never wanted to suffer through that pain, hurt and embarrassment again in life.

Top: Mr. & Mrs. Clifford O. Jarvis, sharing a candid moment at home. *Bottom:* Shorty's older brother, Herbert with his aunt and uncle, Eleanor and Theodore Jarvis, Sr.

Brother Clifford drowned at age 15 at Houghton's Pond, Canton, Massachusetts. Being 12 years of age at the time of his death, I never had time to really get to know him. Brother Donald was one year older than I. He departed this world in 1986, at age 64. During my early years of growing into adulthood, I spent more time with brother Donald than with anyone else in the family. His death was a traumatic experience. In fact, during his funeral services, looking at his sky-blue steel coffin, I said to myself, "But for the grace of the Supreme Power, there go I." It's a very sad, inevitable circumstance of life, to lose the ones you love the most.

Daughter number five was Eva White. She married Sam Smith and gave him three children: Virginia, Anna, and a son, James. Anna and I were born the same year, she one month before me. Although we were first cousins, we always felt like brother and sister. Aunt Eva had a son out of wedlock, named Roger. He and I were closer to each other than most of the family. Roger retired from the United States Army in 1969. He served in both the

Top: **Shorty's sister, Elsie.** *Bottom:* **Shorty's trumpet-playing, honor student brother Clifford who drowned at Houghton's Pond.**

Korean War and Vietnam as a military policeman. Upon retirement from the service he became a Conrail Police Officer. He was also a member of the William E. Carter Post No. 16. While in the service, he also became a member of the Prince Hall Masonic Lodge, Houston, Texas. Roger departed this life at age 52, February 26, 1989. Aunt Eva departed this life June 13, 1994, in Roxbury. She was 94. Incidentally, Aunt Eva was baptized Deaconess Smith of the Union Baptist Church in the year 1911. She was the first female deaconess in our family. She was a very active, faithful church member for 83 years. At the time of her death she was survived by: 11 grandchildren, 30 great-grandchildren, and 16 great, great grandchildren.

Daughters numbers six and seven were Aunt Stella and Aunt Minerva. They passed on early in life; I didn't get to familiarize myself with them: however, I did have the opportunity to both know and to respect them as my aunts. Daughter number eight was Priscilla White. She was better known to the family as Aunt Pree. Her first marriage was to my father's brother, Rufus. Aunt Pree gave Uncle Rufus two children. They were Vera and Theodore. Theodore passed on early in his life, but Vera married Johnny Shelbourne of Roxbury and gave him four children. They were: Janice, Claire, Jackie, and a son, Chucky. Aunt Pree's second marriage was to a Donald King of Harrisburg, Pennsylvania. They had no children. On November 6, 1994, Aunt Pree departed this life at age 94. Uncle Donald left us a few months later. My Aunt Pree and Aunt Eva always

Shorty's brother, Donald, at Monroe Park.

had a big smile on their faces and spoke from their hearts with deep emotions. All praise and thanks to the Supreme Power for permitting me to be a part of this spiritual family. They all contributed so much to my character, personality and spiritual insight to see beyond the apparent, which is, in large part, what this book is all about.

Lastly, I understand Denzel Washington has named his young son Malcolm. For Malcolm X, I thank you Denzel. I believe the naming of your son was a spiritual omen. I also feel it was Malcolm's way of thanking you for your beautiful performance in the movie.

I think it extraordinary that so many memorable events took place in the same months of various years. It has left yet another unforgettable impression on my mind.

Memorable Dates

November 28, 1900	Birth date of my mother, Mrs. Ethel Jarvis
April 17, 1915	The famous singer Billie Holiday was born
September 11, 1923	Malcolm "Shorty" Jarvis born to Ethel and Clifford, Sr.
May 19, 1925	Malcolm Little (later known as Malcolm X) was born
February 16, 1940	I married Hazel Register
February 27, 1946	Malcolm Little and I were sentenced to prison
February 16, 1955	Mrs. Ethel Jarvis passed on. She was my mother. She left us at age 55
February, 1958	Malcolm X married Betty Shabazz
November, 1958	Attilah Shabazz, the first daughter of Malcolm X, was born
November 22, 1963	The J.F.K. assassination took place in Dallas, Texas
February 21, 1965	The assassination of Malcolm X occurred
February 26, 1990	I lost my father, Clifford O. Jarvis, at age 92
February 16, 1992	The *Boston Globe* newspaper published the

2. The Family

	story called, "Malcolm and the Boston Years." The article was written by *Globe* staff reporters Bill Cunningham and Dan Golden
April 10, 1992	I visited the grave sites of Billie Holiday and Malcolm X
November 16, 1992	The world premiere of the movie *Malcolm X* was presented at the Ziegfeld Theater, 141 West 54th Street, New York City
November 12, 1994	Mrs. Pricilla King, my beloved aunt, departed this life at the age of 92
June 1, 1997	Mrs. Betty Shabazz was set aflame by her grandson, Malcolm. She died three weeks later
September 15, 1998	Malcolm "Shorty" Jarvis passed after a five-year battle with prostate cancer

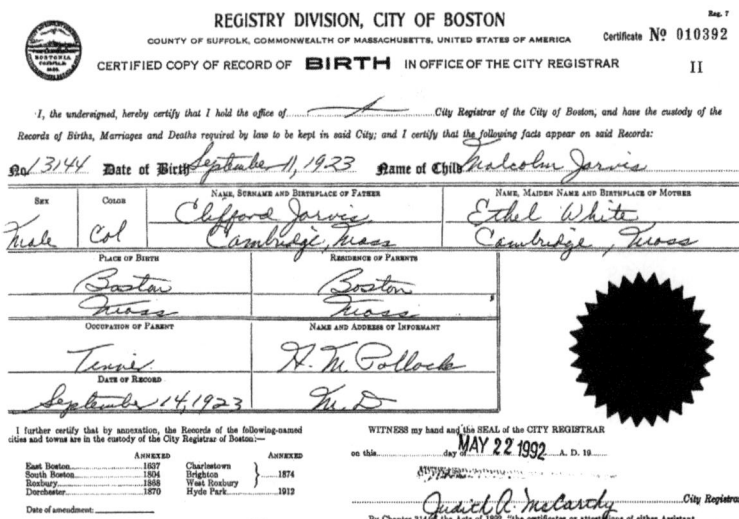

3
Reminiscing

July 14th, 1994: Here I sit at my L-shaped desk, in my swivel chair with a thousand stories pertaining to my personal life and memoirs of the late Malcolm X to tell. My body tenses as my mind starts to wander back through my past life. I find myself reminiscing over unbelievable, incredible incidents.

Houghton's Pond, Canton, Massachusetts, still haunts me after all these years. Brother Clifford was attending a Boy Scout picnic and went swimming with a few companions. He was caught up in a whirlpool undercurrent that took him to the bottom, where he drowned.

Strangely, the day began with fun and excitement and ended in brutal, unforgettable tragedy. This was the year of 1937, July the Fourth. I was 12 at the time, Clifford was 15. I recall a couple years earlier how my father gave Clifford an old trumpet of his. Brother Clifford was an honor roll student attending Boston English High School at the time of his death. Incidentally, father was a professional trumpet player. He was also one of the original charter members of the American Federation of Musicians, Local 535, located then at 409 Massachusetts Avenue in Boston.

For years, I asked my parents to please let me learn to play a saxophone. As a young and very inquisitive boy, I fell in love with the sound of the saxophone. I was later told that instruments were expensive and that my parents could not afford one at the time. When I was 12 years old, disregarding my feelings for the instrument I really wanted, Father shoved my brother's trumpet and his own beginner's book into my hands, saying, "If you desire to play music at all, then stay in the house and practice instead of playing and bike riding."

Coming from my father, I thought that was cold. He didn't understand me or the things I needed as a child. He certainly did not realize that I really wanted to play music, and that as a child, I really needed to let off some steam. One thing that was for sure, I never received any typical father-to-child love from him. I felt later on in my adult life, if he showed more respect and a little warmth and encouragement, I would have turned out differently.

I was an extremely sensitive child who was always very kind and polite to people. During my school years, my ulterior motives were to learn the fundamentals of decent living. My interests lay in music, going to school and satisfying a healthy curiosity about the things I did not know. Taking Father's advice, I studied the music book diligently and practiced my horn long and hard for hours a day. Doing as I was told, resulted in my playing exceptionally well—within a relatively short period of time I was playing like a professional.

At the age of 12, I recall entering an amateur contest at a local dance hall and winning second prize for singing. But playing trumpet made me feel as though I had found an outlet for my pent-up emotions. I can honestly say I put my heart and soul into my music because I felt that I could tell the world many things through musical expression that I could not in words or actions.

Although I was playing well, as yet, I hadn't learned how to read music. I was just playing what sounded good to my ear. At the time, I really didn't care that I could not read music. I was only interested in playing well enough to express my pent-up emotions musically. Eventually, I learned both how to read and to write music.

Being tall and heavy-set made me appear to be older than I was. Although I was only 16, I was admitted to the Musician's Union. What an honor! My admission to the Union at that age happened only because my father sponsored me. I managed to get "gigs" (music jobs) featured as a young "up and comer" with some of the best bands in the City of Boston. For example, I played with the Tasker Crossen Big Band, the Sabby Lewis Orchestra, Herby Lee and many others. In the late thirties and early forties, jazz was booming in Boston. In fact, Boston was world renowned as one of the top three jazz cities in the USA. At the time, there were elegant jazz night clubs in Boston like: the famous Hi-Hat, which used to be located at the corner of Columbus and Mass avenues; Estelle's, was then—and still is—located on Tremont Street; The Old Club Savoy, which was located on upper Columbus Avenue;

Shorty playing the "Celebrity Club" in Providence, Rhode Island, with Herby Lee. *Left to right:* **alto sax, Herby Lee; baritone sax, Willis Lee; trumpet, Malcolm L. Jarvis [1960].**

and Wally's, also located on Mass Avenue, was formerly known as "Little Harlem" and "Club Dixie." Musically speaking, jazz, on the national level, was the most important form of entertainment on the scene of that day. Like rock 'n' roll clubs that abound today, "speakeasies" (jazz clubs) were prevalent then.

I recall also the famous R.K.O. Boston theatre, located downtown on Washington Street, the entertainment center of Boston, and the great Metropolitan theater (now known as the Wang Center). We also had the sophisticated theater for plays, the Shubert, and others. But jazz was king! Jazz clubs were strung all over the city. Everywhere you turned, you were facing a theater or jazz club. The year was 1938, and over the next two years, the late Malcolm X and I would personally meet many of the jazz greats and theater entertainers of the world.

Now that I was a young bona fide member of the Union and owned a car, I was awarded the job of serving as chauffeur for the Union secretary. This position was my pass through the doors of any club, theater, playhouse or establishment of any type of entertainment in the City of Boston. The secretary's basic job was to collect traveling dues from visiting musicians. These dues constituted a tax invoked by the National Federation of Musicians. With jazz at its peak, I couldn't ask for a better opportunity than this one, especially being a black youngster in the racially polarized city of Boston. (The most recent evidence of which was revealed during the early years of bussing in 1974, when the city created a climate that was more like that of Little Rock, Arkansas, of 1957.)

Being on the cutting edge, my success musically made my father very proud. Jazz was on the rise. I was on the rise—what an exciting time to be alive! Within the next four years, I had come of age in the Union. Knowing how to handle myself in the streets, and having my license, helped me to land my new Union job as the Union secretary's chauffeur. My job was interesting because periodically, the secretary would get hassled by musicians who thought he was hassling them. I was there also to keep things on the "up and up."

(I'm sure everyone is familiar with the now famous Max Roach quote on the impact of the wartime entertainment tax on the big bands: that instrumentalists had a war tax at 20 percent, both a city and a state tax. If there was a dancer with the band, there would be 20 percent

A practice session at Shorty's home in Dorchester, Massachusetts. Howard McGee went on to make a name for himself in the 1940s and 1950s. *Left to right:* Mal Jarvis, Walter Radcliffe, Howard McGee.

more tax, 20 percent more for singers, etc. Although these taxes were brutal, most of the musicians respected me. I came to find their major complaint was that the big money-making record companies who were keeping all the rights to their music, most of the royalties, and raking in the big dough should be the ones the secretary should have been going after, not the little man making pennies—and right off the bandstand. They didn't think it showed them respect; besides that, some wanted to know why they weren't trusted to simply mail their dues. In fact, I would discover later, that was one of the major complaints of the 1938 Federal Revenue Act, that it reduced taxes on the large corporations and raised taxes on the smaller companies. Thus, even though it was a national organization, in the larger scope of American business, the National Musician's Union was considered a smaller company based upon its overall revenues, and suffered the same fate as most other smaller companies under this act—they were forced to "up the ante.")

All that aside, this new job was great, because again, along with the secretary of the Union, I would be granted free passes through all the doors of all the concert halls and entertainment spots in Boston. And with jazz at its peak, you couldn't ask for a better opportunity than this one for a black youngster in Boston.

Boston was like a microcosm of the world. At that point in time, the world itself was just as polarized as Boston. While these were the best of times for me, I learned from my chats with many of the visiting musicians that these were also the worst of times on both the national and the world political scenes—even for musicians. On the musical scene, many performers were being blacklisted by the House Committee on Un-American Activities—the most famous black being Eartha Kitt, who's never been able to fully make up the lost ground, to this day.

On the political scene, the world was in upheaval. Russia's threats of invasion, Germany's Nazism, diversionary uprisings by Spanish Nationalists, Italian Fascists and Japanese Imperialism were just a few of the crises threatening the global order. I learned that President Roosevelt's "Fireside Chats" weren't really innocent, naive discussions. I know I never paid any attention to them because I didn't have a working fireplace—nor did most of the people I knew—so I knew he was talking to white folk about white issues. But these musicians "hipped" me to the fact that he was talking about a very politically unstable world, and America's role in helping to both sort out and to straighten things out. They told me I had better pay attention, because if there were a

George Irish—Shorty played with the late George Irish's orchestra from 1951 to 1956.

World War, and if America did decide to enter it, then I'd be included—as a draftee. (By the way—contrary to what is commonly believed, again, I never took glycerin or any other such drug to make my heart sound defective to doctors in order to dodge the draft.)

It was quite an experience at my age to meet, to greet and to associate with international travelers of the entertainment world. This experience expanded my mental horizons tremendously. The influence of the places in which they had performed was reflected in their music. I would like to mention just a few of the jazz greats I was privileged to meet: the great Louis Armstrong, Cab Calloway, Fletcher Henderson, Ivory Joe Hunter, Charlie Barnett, Stan Kenton, Billy Eckstine, Sarah Vaughn, Max Roach, Abby Lincoln, Melba Liston and Dakota Stanton. There was also the great Lionel Hampton, and my main man, Count Basie, who became famous for the profound brass section of his band. When the brass section of the Basie band "hit," it generally would bring those listening right up out of their seats with shock, amazement and excitement.

Yet, I can't forget such greats as the world famous Duke Ellington and the virtuoso members of his orchestra. I became friendly with some of Ellington's featured soloists and side men such as: Johnny Hodges, the lead alto player; Cat Anderson, the screech trumpet player of the band; and Ray Nance, who played the first jazz violin I ever heard.

We would be bolstered by yet another major black female starlet, that year: Ella Fitzgerald singing "A-Tisket, A-Tasket" behind

Sandy Saniford was the piano player with the George Irish group at that time.

The George Irish Orchestra 1952. *Left to right:* trumpets, Bill Douglas and Mal Jarvis; saxophones, Buddy Pearson, Walter Sisco, and the late George Irish (standing); bass (not known), piano, Sandy Saniford.

the incomparable Chick Webb band. This was too much. And, with Hattie McDaniel starring in *Gone with the Wind* (too bad they never took her out of the kitchen), black folk started feeling "kinda important," worthy of respect and praise. It was good reward for a people who had paid their dues many times over, in their recent past. Jazz was our forum. It was our music, and it was being emulated by everyone—though some would accuse it of "wrecking the American home." Well, all that aside, even Glenn Miller got in on the act, forming a big band which would soon become world famous. Jazz was in the air. The joints were jumpin'. Believe it or not, there were many more musicians I met but I can't recall them all.

Mine was a mind-expanding job. Here I was, meeting these musicians who traveled the world and who had all these stories that boggled the mind. I was hearing the influences of the places they'd been, reflected in their music—giving me material to practice up on. Their exposing me to all manner of goings-on beyond my community helped me become open to meeting different kinds of people. One of these people was Malcolm X.

Back in the early forties, he was known as Malcolm Little. He was later known as "Malcolm X," the famous civil rights leader. At times he would use either the alias Jack Carlton or the initials "J.C." From the day I met him, Malcolm always impressed me as being a straightforward, up-front person on all matters pertaining to people, especially

Shorty first met Randy Weston at the Five Spot in Greenwich Village in 1957–58. His oldest son, Clifford Jarvis, was playing drums with Randy at that time.

when speaking to them. We met under rather peculiar circumstances. Although I had been aware of him long before we actually met in person, I was first drawn to him in 1939.

Malcolm had come to Boston to escape a spat of trouble beating down his path in Detroit. He was living at the time at his sister's on 72 Dale Street, in the upper part of Roxbury called "Sugar Hill," where he'd made a reputation for himself. Sugar Hill was where the upper class blacks lived. This class of people was referred to as "The 400 Group," by the black community, much like New York society. There, Malcolm, with a friend, John R., would literally conduct a fashion show merely in their passage up and down Humboldt Avenue. The object of intrigue was their "Zoot Suits." The suits they wore at the time were a replica of the stage outfit worn by the late Cab Calloway, of "Hi-De, Hi-De, Hi-De, Ho!" fame.

The internationally renowned Buddy Pearson.

The suit coat had padded shoulders and was of knee length. The trousers were 32 inches at the knee, and they were tapered to 16 inches at the ankle, presenting a rather baggy, balloon-like, visual impression. I was awe-struck. What a fashion statement, and at the tender age of 14—even though Malcolm looked like he was 20 years of age. From a distance, I admired his "savoir faire," for months before eventually meeting him.

At the time (1939), at 16 years of age, I was still living with my parents on Waumbeck Street, in Upper Roxbury. Around the corner, on Humbolt Avenue, was a poolroom facing Hollander Street. Again,

I always looked far older than my 16 years—as did Malcolm his 14 years. Malcolm was taller than I was. His hair had turned red from "conking," and he had already acquired the name "Detroit Red." Even at that time, he didn't particularly care for the use of his last name in public. He preferred to be called "Red" or "Detroit Red." His shady wheeling, dealing and con artist scheming at all times forced him to encourage the use of nicknames in place of his real name. All this I knew about him before I met him. Being somewhat of a local celebrity myself, I knew that it was just going to be a matter of time before the momentous event occurred.

I was a typical teenager. When I wasn't working, I entertained myself by playing pool. Poolhalls of the thirties and forties were considered to be like the video arcades of today. Then, it was not uncommon for a mother to warn a son or daughter about hanging out in a pool hall. Shooting pool three to four times a week, I used to win spending money from my side bets. Even at that young age, I was considered a very accomplished player. Were I not playing music, I might have

The late Cecil Young and his quartet at the old Hi-Hat Club located on the corner of Mass and Columbus avenues, in Boston. This picture was taken in the early 1940s. Cecil Young is the second from the left in the photo. The girl in the middle was the hat check girl.

3. Reminiscing

Famous trumpeter with the late Duke Ellington orchestra, is pictured at Jim Connelley's Bar and Grill on Tremont Street, Boston, about 1958. *Left to right:* Young Cat Anderson—son of Cat—Mal Jarvis, sitting with valve trombone, Cat Anderson is third from the right. The others in the photo are not known.

gone on the national billiards circuit—and done well. I was well-known and well-respected by everyone who played in this particular poolroom.

As I said before, I met Malcolm under rather strange circumstances. On that particular day, I was in the pool hall, playing the game of my life. The stakes were very high—about 10 percent higher than normal for this kind of game, because of the players—and the pressure was almost unbearable. Malcolm walked in and saw that all the activity that day was around my table. Apparently, he knew of both me and the person I was playing because he immediately began bet-making while he remained totally absorbed in the game. He not only seemed to be studying the table placements and the shots; he also seemed to be studying the players as well.

What I found most intriguing about Malcolm on that day, was that he, a newcomer, was just as much of a celebrity as was I in the city of my birth. And in the pool hall, in the relatively short time he was in Boston, Malcolm had managed to match my level of notoriety as well. For, as he entered, he was greeted by all coming through the door.

Matthew Gee, then a famous trombone player at Storyville in downtown Boston, with the late Duke Ellington Orchestra. The actual photo was taken at a Sunday afternoon jam session at Jim Connelley's, the famous Boston club, located on Tremont Street. In the background is Jimmy Tyler.

"Hi Red! How're you doing?..."
"What's goin' on, Detroit?..."
"Detroit Red...What cha know good?..."
"Cool Daddy-O, what's going down?"
With a short smile, all he said was, "Hi!"

His entrance caused such a stir, I was distracted, momentarily. I looked up from the table with a quick glance. Not knowing him well enough to greet or to speak to, I said nothing. In effect, he was greeted by everyone, except me.

I recall that shot I was about to take during Malcolm's entrance was nearly impossible to make. I had to jump three balls and bank the eight ball into a corner pocket, making it travel the length of the table in the process. The general consensus was that I could not make it. Bets escalated against me. Again, I was disturbed by his entrance.

I was wearing an expensive Longine wristwatch with a brown leather strap. It cost what in today's market would be what close to the equivalent of a Rolex. All eyes were on me, awaiting my decision and shot. I struck the ball at an acute angle, causing it to jump over the obstructing balls and hit the eight ball with enough force to cause the eight ball to bank and roll slowly across the entire length of the table, and to fall with a thud of expended energy into the opposite corner pocket. Those who bet against me lost their money. The entire pool hall went up in a roar. I received a rousing ovation.

During the excitement, the strap on my watch broke. I did not feel the watch fall from my wrist. After the bet payoff, and the cooling down of the excitement, I noticed I'd lost my watch, and was ripping mad.

Shorty at the time he had first met and associated with Malcolm X.

"Did anyone see my watch on the table?" I asked.

The room became catacomb still. To my knowledge, this was the first time Malcolm had ever visited the poolroom. Being a newcomer, knowing of his reputation, and noticing an aggravating smirk on his face, I asked him.

"Did you see my watch fall to the table during that shot?"

Still, with that sarcastic smirk on his face he replied very simply, "No, man…"

That did it. I lost control. In my mind, I knew he took the watch. Everybody else in the pool hall knew and respected me. Nobody else would have taken it. Very quickly, with my left hand I grabbed him by his shirt collar. While drawing back my right fist to hit him, someone grabbed my wrist, stopping me. A male patron who said he'd witnessed the whole thing told me,

"He didn't take your watch," the patron cautioned.

"Well, it sure didn't grow feet and walk. Someone must have it," I said.

"Malcolm didn't take the watch. The person who took it disappeared just that fast out the door," the patron said.

Malcolm appeared unruffled by the entire episode. I was impressed by how composed he was—under the circumstances. I would learn later that Malcolm believed in never letting your enemy see you sweat.

Feeling pretty foolish for my rash behavior, I proceeded to straighten out his shirt, apologizing humbly. Malcolm graciously accepted my apology, and that was the beginning of our lasting and now legendary friendship.

There was so much that we got into, I could not possibly recount it all in two or three books. Oddly, I remember it all as if it were just yesterday. It was those experiences which I trust will help shed some insight as to who we were and the kinds of things we were up to at that time—which led to our eventual incarceration.

One day, while I was walking with Malcolm near the Condon street school in Roxbury, I had an argument with a white fellow. It escalated into a fight. The fight went on for all of two hours. It was a toe to toe battle. (I've often wondered where I got all that youthful energy—although I'd always been grateful for it when I was on the bandstand at that time.) The fight caused such a ruckus, one of the neighbors called the police. For the first time in a long time, I'd met my match. For some reason or other, I just couldn't drop this guy—at all.

Something I'll never forget is how the police treated Malcolm and me after they arrived. They pushed us against a brick wall, let the white boy go and proceeded to question us.

"What's your name?" one of the cops asked Malcolm.

"Malcolm Little..." Malcolm replied.

"And your name?"

"Malcolm Jarvis..." I answered.

"What? Are you guys a couple of smart-alecs?" Grabbing both of us at the same time, the police banged our heads together.

"Hey! I know both of them. That is their true names!" Someone hollered at the policeman.

"If I catch you fighting again, I'll arrest you. Well ... nobody got hurt, so get out of here!"

People would later say that I got Malcolm into that trouble. But by and large, Malcolm admired me for my fighting abilities, having pugilistic tendencies himself. Malcolm was a fighter from the word go. Contrary to popular opinion, Malcolm was a very good boxer. In a minute flat, he could deck the average street thug. (How else do you think he could survive the streets of New York City and run with the Dutch Shultz gang?)

When I was 17 going on 18, Malcolm got a job with Amtrak working the Boston to Washington, D.C., corridor. He worked in the diner car as a sandwich salesman. (Although on the job they called him a sandwich "boy," I would not bring myself to do such. Whenever we were together, we were living the lives of men, not teens. He was such a great con artist, I knew no white adult male on Madison Avenue could touch his skills—at 15. He'd earned the right to be called "salesman," because that is exactly what he was.) He became quite busy. From that point on, whenever he was in town, we'd get together.

Another incident I recall which started innocently and escalated into violence began at Franklin Park one warm summer evening. We decided one night to take our girlfriends for a walk in the park. His girl was Gloria. Malcolm really thought the world of her. She was someone very special in his life, although a serious love connection did not materialize. My girl was Hazel Register, who later became my wife. She lived at 2741 Washington Street, opposite Washington Park. (During the days we played in that park, we never dreamed one day that it would be named after Malcolm X.) I was 15. She had character that stood out in every feature of her face. Her personality was one which displayed all the fine qualities of a highly sophisticated and emotionally mature person with a beautiful soul. Her inner beauty, combined with her external and physical beauty, made her the most charming and captivating girl in our town. She looked like a Japanese doll. Everybody who knew her admired her greatly. Even strangers who passed her on the street were so charmed by her beauty that she would stop traffic. Shortly after meeting her, Hazel became my steady girlfriend. As a loving couple, the first thing I noticed about us was that we got along very well together. For the first time in my life, I could get along with someone else.

I remember so well how I used to visit Hazel and sit with her in the parlor of her home and romance for hours. We would tell each other intimate things we wouldn't dare breathe to any other living soul. This is how we came to know each other so well.

In the year 1941, Hazel became my wife, she at the age of 16 and I at the age of 17. In two years time we had two lovely baby sons. Now for a young couple to be married and to have two children before either of them was 20 years old is, in my opinion, accepting big responsibilities very early in life.

It was a hot summer's night and very dark in the park. Finding a nice grassy spot, we spread our blankets. Sipping our sodas, we commenced to relax. We were only about ten feet from each other. Suddenly, coming over to me, Malcolm said, "Jarvis, we have a Peeping Tom spying on us behind that tree over there."

Hazel Muriel Register, Shorty's first wife and mother of his two sons, Malcolm Jr. and Clifford III.

The girls became nervous and wanted to leave.

"No!" we said. We decided to catch this Tom and to teach him a lesson about invasion of privacy.

Sneaking around opposite ends of the tree, we grabbed the man at the same time. Malcolm hit him in the head from the left. Simultaneously, I hit him in the head from the right. He went down like a tree struck by lightning. We left him there as we split from the scene.

Another brush with the law occurred at Wally's Paradise. "Wally's," as we called it, located on Massachusetts Avenue, was a well-known, black-owned jazz club and a frequent hangout of ours. One Saturday night while we were there, this black woman who had too much to drink was causing a big disturbance. The club owner asked her to leave. She refused. Going outside the club, he called for assistance from a white cop standing near a call box at the corner.

It was about 11:30 P.M. The club was packed with people. The band was swinging and excitement hung thick in the air. Everyone was having the time of their life. Most of the club patrons were black; only a few were white.

When the cop entered the club, he began speaking very nastily towards this black woman, shoving her to the floor because she didn't move fast enough. Not giving her time to get up, he grabbed her by her hair with the intention of dragging her outside. This scene infuriated Malcolm and me to the point of action—cop or no cop. To my surprise, Malcolm approached the cop.

Dotty, Shorty's second wife, the former Dorothy Hurd.

"Take your hands off this woman. If she were your mother or sister, you wouldn't handle her in that manner," he said.

"Mind your own business!" the cop replied as he reached for his gun.

"It's all right. I have one of those, too." Malcolm's hand was already in his overcoat pocket.

While all this action was taking place, I walked up to the cop from behind, bumping into him purposefully to signal that Malcolm was not all alone. I don't remember when we acquired and started to carry guns, but my right hand was in my breast, meaning I had a gun, also. Quickly surveying the situation, the police officer dropped the woman and ran out of the club to the call box to get some backup. We had displayed very bold action for two young black men in the forties, anywhere.

Picking the woman up, we rushed her outside to a cab at the curb, instructing the driver to take her home. I handed the cab driver a ten dollar bill. We left in a hurry before police backup arrived. It was later said the police were looking all over the area for us. Although we were long gone, we were not so soon to be forgotten by the club patrons. They talked about that incident for weeks. The general consensus was, "Detroit Red" and his buddy had the nerve to stand up to a white cop. If the truth be known, it was luck that we didn't get into serious trouble over that incident.

We sensed the police would have undercover detectives watching Wally's, so we didn't plan to go there anytime soon—especially since the cop had included in his report, "Two Niggers carrying guns..." In a few weeks we would consider the coast clear enough to go out again and have some fun—but not at Wally's.

To make a long story short, being known as a Musician's Union employee, and Malcolm being my "Ace Boon Coon," we could select any club as our club of choice. I was Malcolm's ticket into any club door. In fact, this is how he and I met all the big-named people in show business—especially musicians. Again, we met both the big band leaders I'd mentioned earlier and members of their bands, very famous people. The club we chose that day was the Club Savoy. The Savoy was just a few blocks up the street from Wally's—on Massachusetts Avenue. We didn't figure the law was still looking for us. That's why we chose a club so close to Wally's.

The Sabby Lewis Orchestra was appearing. Malcolm wanted to meet Sabby and the band members, consisting then of: Maceo O., Brian and Eugene Caines on trumpets; Ricky Pratt, "Big Bill" Dorsey and a fellow everybody knew as "Jerry" on saxophones; Joe Booker on drums; Al Morgan on bass; and, of course, Sabby Lewis on piano. What a band!

Shorty, just after his third marriage—to Bernice Joyner.

Each member was a star in his own right. Around and about Boston, this band was considered the very best.

Mr. Detroit Red was the center of attraction wherever he went. The cumulative residual effect of his flamboyant zoot suits, bright red, conked hair, wide brim hats and his impeccable grooming was a rare treat anyone would remember—let alone his incredible dancing. I don't know where Malcolm learned to dance (although I suspect it was at house parties), but he "sho 'nuff could cut up some rug."

Well, this Friday was no exception. The house was packed. The band was popping. The trumpets were blazing away. The people, caught up in the excitement, were laughing, talking, dancing, toasting, just having a grand old time as we walked in. Yet, despite the fervor of the moment, as we walked in, all heads turned our way. What a feeling our celebrity status would give us at moments like this one.

Malcolm and I were graciously seated, and drinks were ordered. As our drinks arrived, so did three white girls. They were dressed with such style and class—wearing those new nylon stockings and all—that everybody in the club turned their attention away from us and onto these girls. It just so happened that the only seats available were opposite us at the same table. After being seated, one of the girls pulled out a cigarette. Before she could reach back into her bag, my lighter was at her cigarette.

"Thanks very much," she said, following a couple puffs.

In the meantime, she and Malcolm were eyeballing each other, intensely.

"Hi, my name is Shorty, and this is my illustrious friend, 'Detroit Red.'" Upon my introduction, Malcolm moved his chair closer to the girl he was eyeing, for conversation.

Her name was Beatrice B. We called her "Bea," for short. Bea's girlfriend was Cora M., and the young pretty girl was Bea's 16-year-old sister, Joyce, who was tagging along with her big sister just for the excitement. I knew at a glance these girls were out of place at the Savoy. Their type usually went to the Hi Hat Club on Columbus Avenue, on the corner of Massachusetts Avenue. When "high-class" whites were looking for a good time in the black community, they never came to the Savoy or to Wally's.

We zeroed in on them. We did not want to let them escape us. I started with a jive conversation, trying to make an impression.

"You must have been a beautiful baby!" I said. Everybody laughed.

Malcolm followed up with his bit, creating the impression that we were talent scouts looking for artists.

"Yes, Jarvis! I'm flying back to LA tomorrow. I will inform you of the big discussion as soon as possible!" he remarked.

With the impression made, and the groundwork laid, the bait swallowed whole, and the evening drawing to a close, we were invited to

Shorty, with his fourth bride, Elizabeth English-Jarvis.

Bea's home for collations. (This invitation would grow into a weekly event.) Over time, I noticed Bea and Malcolm became serious about one another. He didn't seem worried that she was married. For that reason, she didn't pose a threat to his freedom. In fact, Malcolm still managed to come and go and to do as he well pleased. Bea, on the other hand, had fallen madly in love with Malcolm. Although it looked to me like love at first sight on Bea's part, I know for a fact, that on Malcolm's part the feeling was not mutual. (Whereas Malcolm was sexually involved, my relationship with these white girls was purely platonic. At the time, I was dating three black girls in and around the Boston area. As a result, I was not interested in an affair with any of Bea's friends or family. I had my hands full already.)

Bea's husband was a traveling salesman who made very good money. Maybe that's what attracted her to Malcolm—his natural, raw sales ability. Her husband was away from home, three to four weeks at a time. Of our entire entourage, the only sexually involved couple was that of Malcolm and Bea. Her husband drove a big Cadillac and we wanted to use it. But she feared one of her husband's friends would spot her and a black man in his Cadillac. Now, I always stayed with a very nice car. Invariably, I would refer to any car as my "short," because cars shortened the distance between two points.

"Let's use my short, for safety's sake," I volunteered. On that day, Malcolm nicknamed me "Shorty," and referred to me as such from then on.

By this time, we'd decided to form a small gang as a way of making these rendezvous pay off, or making them more financially productive for all parties involved. We added two new members: John R. and Sonny B. Sonny B. had a yen for Cora M., but nothing ever materialized.

At this time, his work on the train brought him to many cities. Malcolm, in some of the cities he visited, started making alliances well beyond our gang—and with some rather notoriously shady characters. Occasionally, he would have to lay over. On one such occasion, he had to lay over in New York City, to rest. Whenever he stayed over in the city, it was with a friend of his named Sammy McNight. Sammy was in the New York numbers rackets. When Malcolm would visit Sammy, he'd spend his time hustling up spending money by picking up numbers for racketeers who worked for the Dutch Schultz crime family. They were very heavy hitters—literally.

One incident I remember so well was that one day someone hit a four-way number. The syndicate's payoff to Malcolm's party was $2,000. Two thousand dollars at that time was a whole lot of money—and, in the hands of a teenager, too tempting to handle. That much money in one lump sum looked so good, Malcolm couldn't see paying it to the player. Instead, he had Bea take a train to "The City" and they spent a week at the Victoria Hotel.

Likewise, I had moved along in my life. I had married and separated from my longtime girlfriend, Hazel Register, leaving her with two children. As my married life moved along, I continually nagged and argued with my wife as most men do. Yet I loved her to the extent that I worshipped the ground she walked on. After years of putting up with my evil disposition, she finally concluded that a separation would be the best thing for both of us. (As I recollect my past life, I see where I was tragically wrong. I was so busy looking for my wife, and anyone who came in contact with me, to give me their sympathy and understanding, that I failed to do unto them as I would have them do unto me. I sincerely believe Hazel left me for my own benefit, not hers or the children's. The fact that she would never consent to a divorce proves to me that she loved and understood me better than I understood myself. She later told me she only left me in hopes that a separation would help me

Clifford, III, and Malcolm, Jr., enjoying their dog in the back yard.

to find myself that much sooner. Then we could reunite and resume our lives in happiness once again.) This situation left me with the apartment at 4 Hollander Street all to myself. Late one night my phone rang. It was Sammy, a friend in New York City.

"Jarvis, you come and get your buddy out of New York, and now, or you will read about him," he said.

"What's wrong?" I asked.

"He failed to make a payment of a lot of money for a hit, and a contract is out on him," Sammy replied.

Not having heard from Malcolm in some time, I didn't know what to believe, but knowing Malcolm must be in trouble, I responded, "I'll be there first thing in the morning."

Sammy lived up off Edgecomb Avenue, near St. Nicholas Avenue. The next morning at seven o'clock, sharp, I was ringing on Sammy's doorbell. A sweet, soft voice responded through the intercom.

"Who is it?"

"Jarvis! I'm looking for Sammy."

A few moments later the door swung open. An absolutely gorgeous, coppertoned woman greeted me.

Shorty and his teenage sons, Clifford, III, and Malcolm, Jr., "steppin' out."

"I'm Hortense, Sammy's girlfriend," she said.

At the same moment, Sammy came to the door, handing me a small bag saying, "Hi Jarvis, this is all Red has here. Go park near the corner of St. Nicholas and Edgecomb, outside the Club La Marr–Cheri. He'll show up there, sooner or later."

The La Marr–Cheri was both a club and a restaurant, which served breakfast through the night. Most mornings Malcolm ate breakfast there. This particular morning, I did not know what to expect. Was he alive? Dead? Who was he traveling with? Who's after him? Do they know how he looks? Was there a tail on him at that moment? How dangerous a situation was I in? Puffing on my cigar while waiting, those were some of the thoughts which ran through my mind. Sure enough, in a matter of minutes, I noticed Malcolm strolling down the street. I rolled down the car window and yelled to him.

"Hey! What's up, man?" Malcolm's face lit up like a Christmas tree.

"Jarvis! am I glad to see you!" he yelled back.

"Yes, I thought you would be," I said.

"Hit the road, now. Don't even go by Sammy's for my things," he added.

"I have them," I said, lifting the bag. On the way back to Boston, he explained everything.

"I spent two thousand dollars on Bea that didn't belong to me. It was a number payoff. The people due the money reported it to the racketeers. They put out a contract on me. That's why I had to get out of there as soon as possible. You know Jarvis, you're probably saving my life."

"I know. That's what friends are for. A friend in need is a friend indeed." We joked and otherwise enjoyed a rather pleasant ride back to Boston.

Upon arriving in Boston, Malcolm warned, "I don't think I should stay at my sister's as a precaution. The gangsters might trace me from people who know me well in the city."

"You can stay at my house. I have two bedrooms," I suggested.

I estimate Malcolm lived in my house almost a year. For that year, we were like peas in a pod. Whenever you saw him, you saw me. In fact, Bostonians at large started associating us with each other. But the Malcolm that returned with me to Boston was not the same Malcolm who had left. His experiences had changed him. His crime activity had escalated. He was willing to risk more and more, as time went on.

One cold winter night, we made a reservation for five people at the Savoy Club. The reservation was for the three girls, Malcolm and me. About 10 o'clock, the girls arrived in a cab. We were there to greet them. Bea, who didn't like gloves, was wearing a Russian puff to keep her hands warm.

It felt like a lifetime had passed since the incident with the policeman at Wally's. We never thought the law would still be looking for us, "gun-toting," would-be "cop killers." They weren't—except for one black detective named Harvey Yates. Detective Yates was so mean and nasty, he lived in perpetual fear for his life—although he didn't act like it. He was known to be the type of cop who would build a reputation for himself at the expense of innocent people. Word on the street was that someone had taken a couple of shots at him. That is why he wore a bulletproof vest—always.

We were having a drink when in walked Detective Yates, heading straight for our table. Malcolm passed his gun under the table to Bea. Adorned with his vest, Detective Yates preened. Yelling, to gain the attention of the attendant patrons, he demanded of Malcolm, "Red, stand up!"

Mr. Yates then proceeded to frisk Malcolm in a very rough manner, from head to toe. He seemed to have no intention other than to embarrass us in the presence of the white girls. He was good at his job—especially when it involved harassment of any kind. On this occasion, he'd be disappointed. Finding nothing after getting the attention of all the patrons in the club that night, we embarrassed him.

"O.K., you can sit down," Yates ordered, and walked away.

Once again, Lady Luck smiled on us. For had I been asked to stand and were I subjected to a frisking, I would have been caught red-handed with my gun.

"If he had tried to arrest you, I was going to shoot him," Bea said to Malcolm.

I didn't know, but Bea had the gun under the table in her puff and aimed at Yates' midsection. When she told us, both of us realized just how close that one was. We broke out into a cold sweat. I turned to Malcolm, "Is Bea that much in love with you?" I asked him.

"Yes, I guess she is," he said with a smile.

Observing the way he handled this incident, Malcolm had taught me a serious lesson about street smarts. He never let an opponent observe fear in him. In fact, he was smiling in Yates' face the whole time he was being frisked and patted down. I admired his courage in the face of danger. This incident calls to mind yet another courageous brush with death, in which Malcolm held his ground without "lettin' 'em see him sweat."

There were two gambling houses we frequently used: Johnny McGovain's and George Holt's. McGovain's was the prostitutes' late night hang out. There, they would wait for a lucky winner to buy some of their time. Johnny kept clean rooms for hire—for the prostitutes, only. Malcolm and I gambled for money, not prostitutes. For that reason we didn't particularly care for McGovain's place. Holt's house was our place of choice for gambling. There were no women present, just men, greedy for money.

One evening after we had robbed a few houses, we had in our possession a case of scotch we had taken from one of those houses. Although I preferred top-shelf cognac, Malcolm liked Johnny Walker Scotch, Black Label. He had been sipping all day, and by nightfall he felt no pain. Usually, he held his liquor exceptionally well, but not this night. Not being in his normally sharp mental condition to gamble, Malcolm went broke and took on an attitude. In the past, he had lost, borrowed money from George, and paid it back the next day. Assuming his credit still good, he inquired of Holt, "Holt, loan me a couple hundred until tomorrow?"

An Italian gangster from the North End of Boston banked the game for George. Sitting on the table was a bank of $5,000 in cash. Holt's reply to Malcolm's request was an outright, "NO!" short and nasty.

"You've had enough to drink. Leave and come back when you're sober," Holt added.

Ripping mad, shoving his chair back from the table and coming to his feet, Malcolm said, "If I can't gamble here tonight, then nobody will."

Malcolm tossed two guns onto the table, then put his hand into the breast of his coat, giving the impression he had another gun. Speaking loudly he said, "Let the baddest person here reach for one."

The Italian banker snatched up the bank roll and shoved it into a paper bag, saying, "George, this is it for tonight." Then he left.

Sonny B., John R. and I were carrying guns. We surrounded Malcolm to protect him in the event of any occurrence. Furiously, George screamed, "Red, I can't have you disrupting my business, especially on my busiest night. The next time you come, you check your guns with me or don't come in. I'm not joking."

About this whole event, what I didn't understand is why Malcolm would first of all provoke these men, then put his hand into the breast of his coat. He had two guns only, and he threw them onto the table. My guess is, he depended on the three of us for protection, and we gave it to him. That was the last time I laid eyes on George Holt—before going to prison. Since that time, both he and McGovain have expired. However, that was yet another instance of Malcolm's never letting 'em see him sweat—even in a drunken condition. It was amazing!

All would soon come crashing down. Our affiliation with these white girls would soon lead to our eventual demise; less because of what we did, more as a result of society's disdain for our group's interracial makeup.

At this point, his luck having gone bad and being broke, Malcolm took a watch (stolen from one of our gang's job locations) and pawned it. The watch was an expensive Rolex. I believe it was worth over $1,000. At that time, $1,000 was a lot of money. Not thinking, he took it to a pawnshop on Dudley Street—of all places. He really loved that watch and didn't want to part with it. He told the pawnbroker he would be back in a day or two to retrieve it. That was his mistake.

In the meantime, detectives from the Boston Police Headquarters had distributed to the city's pawnshops a stolen property list from several of the locations we'd hit. The owner of the Dudley Street Pawnshop notified the police once he found a match for Malcolm's watch on the listing. He told them, "The party would be picking it up, anytime."

Immediately, the police put on a stakeout at the pawnshop. A day later, Malcolm went to pick up the watch. Four detectives were waiting for him. They arrested him without a struggle.

After his initial arrest, Malcolm was taken to Boston Police Headquarters. In his possession were two guns and two address books. While he was being photographed and fingerprinted, his address books were looked through and the names of the three girls and me were revealed. December 15, 1945, was the date of Malcolm's arrest. I was arrested four days later.

My occupation at that time was as a sandwich salesman on the Boston to Buffalo, New York, train. At that time, I was working 44 hours a week for 40 cents an hour. (That was the prevailing minimum wage.) This particular night while I was at work, the detectives came to my parents' home at 78 Waumbec Street and presented a search warrant to them. (A month or so before our arrest took place, I had moved back in with my parents—from 4 Hollander Street.) The house, when searched, produced one bullet—found in my bureau drawer. Upon finding the bullet, it was assumed I was armed and dangerous.

I never carried a gun to work. I kept it inside the doors of my mother's player piano. I knew no one in the house would think of that as a hiding place, not even the police. They searched the house and found nothing. My train was on its way back to Boston, from Buffalo. At the Framingham, Massachusetts, stop, the police boarded the train looking for me. My chores completed ahead of time, I went forward to an empty seat to relax in the next car. Three men passed by me, heading to the dining car. Moments later, upon my return, two of them passed me again. The third one spied me lying down in the seat. Beckoning to the other two, they surrounded my seat. The one nearest me gave me a poke asking, "Are you M. Jarvis?"

"Who wants to know?" I asked. My response was answered with yet another question.

"Do you know a Malcolm Little?"

Feeling nasty because I had been disturbed, and knowing something to be wrong upon hearing that question, I became quiet.

"Do you have some ID? If so, let me see it," I was then told.

I threw my coat back quickly, reaching for my back pocket. All of the detectives jumped back from my seat preparing to draw their guns—

the assumption being I was armed and dangerous. To everyone's relief, I pulled out my wallet. After the ID check, I was told, "You are under arrest for breaking and entering in the nighttime."

I was smart enough not to volunteer any information at this point, lest I further incriminate myself. At police headquarters I was asked, "Where is your gun?"

"I don't own one," I answered.

"Well, we found a bullet in your house. There must be a gun to go with it," said the officer.

"That does not mean that I own a gun. In fact, that bullet is a souvenir given to me by a friend from the service," I replied. To this day there has never been any proof that I owned a gun.

I was asked no further questions but was locked up in the Middlesex County Jailhouse in Cambridge, Massachusetts. When my father paid me a visit, I told him where to find the gun and asked him to dispose of it in the Charles River. Because the girls were white, the cops wanted to literally crucify Malcolm and me. But they couldn't pin a gun on me. Therefore, I couldn't be charged with breaking and entering with a dangerous weapon. Being armed was considered a very serious offense, and carried a 20-year prison term. Malcolm was caught with two guns in his possession and charged with illegal possession of a firearm. (It was never proven in court that guns were displayed while the crimes were being committed, so neither of us had to do big time.) Not satisfied with the light gun charges, they tried to get us from yet another angle.

The D.A. and the detectives tried to pressure the girls into saying they were raped. Knowing it not to be true, the girls would not tolerate the idea—especially since they had recently learned that it would have meant 20 years to life for us if they gave in to these underhanded tactics. As first offenders, our sentence should not have been more than one year probation. It seems our biggest crime was being born black and associating with white women. The court didn't seem too interested in the crimes. They seemed more concerned with our skin color, vis-à-vis our activities.

(Where did I get this idea? I recall that during the time when I attended school, I had no problem with race or skin color. The school consisted of 1,500 white students and about 20 blacks. I dated girls of all races, creeds and colors. If I liked a person and they in turn liked me, nothing else mattered, certainly not what people thought. My inner search for self, coupled with a positive sense of self-esteem, encouraged my association with people other than my own race. The problem was, the prejudiced minds of the general public at that time wouldn't tolerate such an open approach to life—and these self-same individuals were the ones condemning Hitler and his hatred of the Jews, not that he didn't deserve condemnation. At this time in my life, I'd become infatuated with white people and their lifestyle, while forgetting my skin was black. Thinking white and being black proved detrimental for me, and was a decisive factor in my treatment at the trial and later incarceration.)

In reminiscing over the aforementioned activities, I've come to see how preordained events seem to have had a way of occurring in Malcolm's and my life. But we were too preoccupied with playing inner-city survival games, and we missed their introduction, no matter how strange they appeared in light of all the other things we were doing. Yet, the objective of these events was meant to be made manifest to us, and by all means it was. In fact, throughout the stories I've told, I now see a guiding hand—a Guardian Angel, if you will—steering us clear of real danger and arresting the hand of our pursuers from curtailing our lives in our greatest hours of need, while directing us to the light of truth and to a higher calling in life.

Another strange, preordained event occurred at this time in a very "down-home," concrete way, through another visit from my father. Malcolm and I awaited trial in the Middlesex County Jail, in Cambridge, Massachusetts, for almost three months. On this visit, my father left me a copy of the King James version of the Holy Bible. He said, "Son, read the Bible and get down on your hands and knees and pray to Jesus Christ as God." Strange as it may sound, I took Dad's advice and read the Bible from cover to cover.

For 45 days and nights I prayed and prayed and prayed some more. When I wasn't on my hands and knees, I was reading the Bible. I can truthfully say while I was at liberty I was not the best Christian I could have been, yet I attended church somewhat regularly. But during those 45 days and nights of awaiting trial, I prayed diligently to Jesus Christ as God and asked Him for redemption in a prayer of my own that went like this: "Oh Lord, oh Lord, please hear my sad and humble plea. I am not the criminal that these people who represent the law believe and would have others believe. I pray to thee, oh Lord, to please send me home. Please give me this one and only chance to prove to everybody that I am not bad, but good—with a good heart. Please, oh Lord, send me home for the sake of my two baby sons who would really be the ones to suffer if I am kept in prison. I thank Thee, oh Lord. I thank Thee, from the bottom of my heart for listening to my humble pleas."

Yet another one of those aforementioned preordained events occurred with my meeting a strange and powerful man just before going to jail. Originally from India, Abdul Hameed, an Ahmadiyyan Muslim, was instrumental in both Malcolm's and my life. He was a very distinguished-looking man; well built and weighing about 220 pounds, he wore a black fez with a long black tassel and a neatly trimmed beard. He looked Asian in some ways, and walking around Roxbury in that attire (like Malcolm's zoot suit) he attracted a lot of attention. Prior to my arrest, I was attracted to him, and one day introduced myself as a young musician and trumpet player.

Talking with Mr. Hameed, one thing led to another. I was eventually invited to his home for further and deeper discussion. Abdul Hameed's house was in the same neighborhood as Johnny McGovain's gambling house on Hammond Street. It was around the corner from McGovain's on 56 Windsor Street.

On my first visit to Abdul's house, he presented me with both a lecture and a concert of classical music. He owned an eight foot, Masson Hammond concert grand piano. All my life I had never heard a finer quality of sound from a piano. When the inspiring concert was over, Abdul introduced me to books on Oriental history and philosophy from both India and Egypt. He also showed me some books on harmony and music composition and theory. I felt like I was receiving a college education in one visit. I knew I had to introduce Malcolm to this gentleman.

Getting Malcolm to meet Abdul Hameed was a difficult task. Being totally absorbed in the "dog-eat-dog" world of hustling where only the fittest survived, Malcolm did not want to hear talk of religion or education—especially coming from me, his running buddy, his partner in crime. After numerous suggestions, eventually Malcolm consented to meet Mr. Hameed.

After meeting Malcolm, Abdul took great interest in us and spent many hours teaching us. He thought we deserved a better way of life than the one we were living. It was Abdul Hameed who presented us our first mention of Islam—his point of view being based on the Ahmadiyyan movement originating in India.

As a Christian, I listened out of curiosity. From childhood, being a musician, I've always had an open mind and wanted to learn about things of which I had no knowledge. Even though Malcolm and I would later hear of Islam—during our incarceration—from Elijah Muhammad (who I consider Malcolm's Pygmalion), our introduction to Islam came from Abdul Hameed. (In fact, I believe the first mention of Islam came to Boston during the early 1940s via the Ahmadiyyas.) Upon his release from prison, Malcolm would later go on to introduce Mr. Muhammad's version of Islam to Boston in 1952.

Still, another strange but true incident which happened to me around this time involved a close friend of Abdul Hameed's named Rashee. He too was from Egypt. Rashee was the only name by which I knew this gentleman to be called. He was tall, of thin build and as black as the ace of spades.

Again, during my association with Malcolm and the white girls, I kept company with three black girls. One special girl did exist, however. Her name was Jackie Taylor. In my eyes she was "Boss Queen." Of all the women I dated, I became emotionally and spiritually infatuated with Jackie. Plainly speaking, I was deeply in love (and like the popular tune of the time made famous by Coleman Hawkins said), "Body and Soul." Due to a misunderstanding Jackie and I had one day, we severed our relationship. She performed a disappearing act on me. She was nowhere to be found. I became pent-up with frustrated emotions. In discussing my personal problems with Jackie to Abdul Hameed, I broke down and cried like a baby. Having no idea where she was, I worried myself sick. I told Abdul, "No matter what, I want her back. This emotional sickness in the pit of my stomach is unbearable."

"Jarvis, do you really want her back?" Abdul asked.

"Yes!" I said.

"Come with me. I'll take you to someone who will bring her back to you, regardless of where she might be," he said.

"This is some strange stuff. But out of desperation, I will try anything," I thought to myself.

Rashee lived in a small apartment on Washington Street, near the corner of Dover Street. Upon entering the apartment, I noticed a human skull on the table. A lighted candle was inside the skull making its eyes appear "other-worldly," almost functional in some strange way, as the eyes danced upon the wall. I was greeted with a smile and a warm handshake.

The mysterious Jackie Taylor.

"Please, be seated," he said.

After a short conversation about my problem, Rashee made a request, "Bring me three silver dollars and a picture of Jackie as soon as possible."

My initial thought was, he wanted the silver dollars as payment for his services. These thoughts were wrong. That was not the case.

The next day, I returned alone with the things he requested. Rashee was not a conversationalist. Preparing for a ceremony in my presence, I was told, "Please, be very quiet."

Looking at the eyes of the skull, I became a little nervous. Saying a prayer in Arabic, he scribbled Arabic on the picture. Then, he wrapped the silver dollars up with the picture and sealed it with Scotch tape. He gave me my instructions: "Bury the packet in the graveyard, six inches deep, near a tombstone. Your Jackie will be back within two weeks—no matter where she may be."

As strange as it may sound, I received a phone call from Jackie within four days. To my surprise, she came to the house to see me. She claimed she missed me and thought strongly about me. We hugged, kissed and spent a wonderful evening together—even though our differences remained unsettled. She wanted her freedom to live her life as she pleased. Although I loved her very much, I felt the same way. Once again, we parted the best of friends.

Suddenly, just after Jackie left, bad luck befell me. I lost my job and went flat broke. Jackie had come and gone again. I felt as if the bottom had fallen out of my life and the world was about to end for me.

Once again, I related my troubles to Abdul Hameed who sent me back to Rashee. I was advised, "Go back to the graveyard and remove the packet. Unwrap it. Burn the picture and spend the silver dollars."

After doing as I was told, my luck changed immediately.

This incredible story, as strange as it may sound, was very true. It was my first encounter with strange phenomena. Again, being raised a Christian, this episode reminded me of a story that took place in Biblical times. It involved Jesus Christ, Judas Iscariot and 30 pieces of silver. The questions arose in my mind, "What does silver have to do with the dead, living and ceremonial rites?" Why is *it* used instead of some other metallic element?"

I came to learn at so young an age that strange, spiritualistic phenomena occur, daily—and to this day, remain beyond our threshold of understanding. But, lack of comprehension is no grounds for condemnation. For me, it became a stimulant to seek out the truth, as I believed that knowing something is better than knowing nothing, and at this point in my life I wanted to know something. I was beginning to feel I knew nothing at all. In fact, many times I felt as stupid as Billy the Kid—because of the way I was living my life. Little did they know, but my introduction to Abdul Hameed and Rashee had given me a lifetime of food for thought. Though I'm sure they've passed on, in my mind, they live on. And like Bob Hope's now famous closing song of the time, all I can say to all those (both mentioned and not mentioned) who played a role in the development of my life, for better or for worse—especially, Malcolm X—is: "Thanks for the memory."

In closing this chapter, I'd like to admonish those who've read this reminiscence. Prison is not at all as glamorous as it's cracked up to be. Malcolm and I at this time were leading very stupid lives. That's why we got locked up in the first place. The circumstances of our trial left speculation for questions about racist attitudes clouding the justice that was meted out to us. That is the source of my anger with the justice system in my trial and eventual incarceration, not some wild belief that I was innocent of any crime. Let me close with more details as to how painfully those who buy into the current "Gangsta for Life" mentality might suffer through the waste of their greatest resource—the time of their youth—if they don't smarten up and wake up.

In those wild and reckless years from 1939 to 1945, I lost out, ultimately. Where the musicians had begun the great job of introducing me to what was going on around me in the world, I got so caught up in my everyday existence that I paid no attention—after I slipped away from associating with them—and so much transpired. The world was gearing up for war, for one thing. In prison, I would have to learn of this escalating world situation: Hitler's blitzkriegs in Poland and his invasions on other European battlefronts; Japan's "New Order" in the Far East; Russia's invasion of Poland; America's development of an Atomic Bomb, and so on. At that point, I became very patriotic. But, of course, having a criminal record, I couldn't even be drafted when I came of age (at that time the ages were 21–36, and were later dropped to 18 years of age). Even things like watching my children grow up escaped me. I had to experience color television in prison, not at home with my two kids, because up to that time, I'd lived an irresponsible life. I even missed the New York World's Fair.

Finally, being in prison was no badge of honor. There, I had a lot to think about. There, I was confronted by the horrible and frightening specter of myself, and what I had done—and not done, as you will see.

4
Trial and Incarceration

My grandfather told me yet another story once. It went something like this:

"A farmer put a baby pigeon in a chicken coop to be raised as a chicken. When the pigeon finally grew up to its full size, it didn't think about flying away—even though it was always being pecked at by the other chickens in the coop. Finally, the pigeon couldn't take being pecked at any more. He wanted out. It just so happened that a big rooster, 'the cock of the walk,' decided that he was tired of playing with this strange bird. You see, the rooster didn't know if he could trust the pigeon, because the pigeon didn't look like him, act like him, and from what he could see, wasn't like him. So, he was going to either kill him, or to make the pigeon just like him by crippling the pigeon so it could never fly. As the rooster approached, it must have had fire in its eyes because the pigeon knew the rooster meant business. He wasn't coming to invite the pigeon to a cocktail party. The pigeon was frightened for his life. He started to run faster and faster, and as a reflex, he began to flap his wings harder and harder. Soon, his body rose up off the ground, above the chickens. In that instant of panic, the pigeon found out he could fly, and flew the coop—never to return."

One night in jail awaiting trial, as I lay trying to sleep, this thought came to me. For the first time, I was able to see what my grandfather was trying to tell me all those years ago: that I was born a black man to black parents, in a white society, educated in a white school without ever knowing I had been growing up in a racist society and never taught to know my potential. I never knew who I was until these distorted circumstances forced me to make an effort to change. I found a moral to my grandfather's story: "Nothing ventured, nothing gained." In other words (in my case) you will never know the results of a course of action in life—even if it comes as a result of life-threatening circumstances well beyond one's control—unless you take action. And if any one motive can encapsulate the method behind the madness of my ensuing trial, that is it.

The trial was the biggest fiasco I'd ever witnessed in all my days. The saddest feature of it was, it was our trial. All the pretrial publicity, the angst, mental frustration, and confusion while awaiting trial; it felt like I was poorly propped on a shaky fence, on either side of which awaited "outrageous misfortune." I was twisting myself into a pretzel for nothing, building myself up for an awful let-down.

On the one hand, intuitively, Malcolm and I knew the trial would not go in our favor (and that's not because we weren't joining in the national fervor over Irving Berlin's new song, "God Bless America"). We were not singing America's praises at this time. On the contrary, we felt that the American system of justice was flawed and cracked; blind, but not color blind.

On the other hand, the Bible and the daily newspaper was all that we were allowed to read. Again, I anchored myself in the Bible, diligently and thoroughly studying it. I prayed morning, noon and night to Jesus Christ, the only God bred into me from childhood, and bolstered my faith in Christianity. The day of the trial was charging down our path like a raging bull with reckless abandon. Malcolm told me I was wasting my time looking for "brownie points."

"You are their brownie point. If you could go to the gas chamber for this, you'd be cooked before you could finish another 'Our Father,'" Malcolm said.

Finally, the day arrived. We were taken from jail to the courtroom. My mind was overcome by conflicted emotions and the anguish of thinking about the corruption which was getting ready to take place in this "Palace of Justice." Anger, fear and rage swept through me like a gale force wind through a mountain cave.

I heard the clerk of court say in a loud voice, "All rise. This court is now in session. The Honorable Judge Allen G. Buttrick presiding."

Looking around the courtroom I saw people, but I heard nothing. I felt like I was floating in space, like my mind had left me.

We were placed in a steel cage like a pair of animals. Despite our confinement, the scene in the courtroom would become just as wild as the clubs in which we lived our lives. What was both said to us and done to us on that day, by both the district attorney and the arresting officers, I will never forget, as long as I live.

"If we had you Niggers down South, we would hang you. You had no business associating with white women," the D.A. said, prancing back and forth in front of the cage in an arrogant manner. I exploded with fury upon hearing that remark. "You low-life son-of-a-bitch!" I yelled, violently shaking the cage—and I wasn't really a cursing man. (That anger reverberates to this day whenever I hear about cases involving racial prejudice like Rodney King's.) I was so mad, I reached out to grab and hit him. His face blood red with anger, he walked away mumbling to himself. (I could well imagine what he was mumbling.)

Later, Malcolm would ask me, "Why did you do that? Didn't you know that officer was just setting you up to demonstrate to the court the reason why you needed to be caged like an animal, then locked up and you played right into it?"

Well, all I can say is that you had to be there to know the extent to which the deck was stacked against us from the moment we walked into that courtroom. I didn't feel this situation could have been any more injurious or unfavorable. In fact, acting the way I did gave me some release. I'll tell you what, I sure enough knew how Samson felt strapped between those two pillars—and why he didn't care that he died in the rubble. I also knew what political prisoners around the world must have felt like—even though I didn't consider myself a political prisoner. I knew I was a thug, and was proud of my well-earned reputation. Malcolm and I were the "Young Lions" of Roxbury.

Nonetheless, at that time I became perplexed by questions and paradoxes concerning the issue of race—something I had never before considered. After all, I was only 19 years of age. I was haunted each night and tormented each day by questions like: What is wrong with humanity that we are so full of hate and prejudice? Why aren't we more concerned about each other—because if we can't co-exist, then eventually, we won't exist? For example, how was it that at this time we could build an atomic clock that would be accurate to within one second in 3 million years, and yet we couldn't even figure out how to get along with our own brother—especially since, at this time, we were 2 to 3 billion strong, worldwide? Case in point, 800 million children were starving all over the world. Yet, that year in the United States, we threw away more food than most of those starving countries produced in an entire year. Furthermore, what kind of civilization spends its time and money counting three hundred million stars in the Milky Way, but doesn't spend, either a minute or a nickel trying to figure out how to get along with their neighbor across the way?

The judge gave the girls a slap on the wrist—suspended sentences—and freed them. I had a sneaking suspicion they wanted to clear the court to "work out" on the Niggers, like the D.A. insinuated. With the racial hatred that pervaded that courtroom, we knew we were cooked—even though this was our first offense. The girls were accomplices, and all five of us committed those crimes, so all five of us should have been guilty, innocent or suspended together. Despite the fact that we might have done a whole lot more than this one incident in our brief lives of crime, we were being sentenced for only one, "B and E." Again, we too should have been given suspended sentences if the court practiced equality under the Law. Truth be known, these B&E's were the girls' idea. They occurred in the girls' neck of the woods. They were set up by the girls, and yet the girls were being treated like all they did was "slip by," taking a respite on the "wrong side of innocence." They were more guilty than were we. These girls were as tough as "Annie" who got her gun and didn't look back. These were no white goddesses. I guess it's like Rogers and Hammerstein said, "there's nothing like a dame"—but not so in the eyes of the judge and the district attorney.

"You are hereby sentenced to eight to ten years on this account…eight to ten years on that account…eight to ten on this account…" The judge must have repeated these accounts about 14 times.

I was in mental shock. I felt like I had been hit in the head by a blunt instrument and knocked senseless. I felt drugged in some strange way by this verdict. That year, Winston Churchill had introduced the term "The Iron Curtain." Well, it felt like the judge and the district attorney had adorned this courtroom with an iron curtain of injustice, hit us in the head with the iron, wrapped us in the steel curtain and threw us to the sharks. And as I rose from my seat feeling like a person emerging from under anesthesia after a major operation—half in and half out of it—grabbing the bars in an attempt to shake them loose, I screamed at the judge, "Why don't you find me guilty of murder and kill me? I'd rather be dead than to spend my life in prison." (Why the papers did not report completely what I really said, I'll never know.)

The black spectators went berserk. Many had waited to see how our case was going to be handled by the court—especially Malcolm's sister, Mrs. Ella Collins.

"Yes, you people are prejudiced!" Ella hollered at the judge.

"You are sending my boy to prison!" my mother screamed at the judge. The entire group my mother was with started milling towards the judge's bench shouting hysterically and waving their arms. The angry spectators were getting quite restless.

"Clear the courtroom. We will proceed without spectators!" The judge yelled to his deputies.

One deputy grabbed Mrs. Collins by the arm to usher her out. Now, Mrs. Collins was a strong, 185 lb., well-built black woman. She backhanded him across the face for putting his hands on her. With her other hand, she bounced him off the wall with such an impact you would have thought she was "Goliath in drag."

At that point, the judge ordered the riot squad in to quell the angry disturbance. We were taken out of the courtroom to the jailhouse by way of a secret passage behind the judge's bench, for fear the angry crowd would attempt to free us. They wouldn't dare take us through the front door.

Four deputy sheriffs—Charles S. Robbins, Fred Claus, John Johnson and Clarence McElroy—were called to the scene. They made haste in clearing the courtroom. The group continued to demonstrate and to demand readmittance. Three state troopers were also called. The combined law enforcement group finally forced the agitators out of the courthouse. This was justice?

The next day, February 26, 1945, the *Boston Daily Record* carried front page headlines which read: "Rout Kin in the Sentencing of 2":

> One of the wildest demonstrations ever seen in Middlesex Superior Court was staged yesterday. 15 relatives and friends of two Negro youths acted up. The pair had pleaded guilty to participating in a series of housebreaks, with three white girls. They were sentenced to eight to ten year prison terms. After pronouncement of sentence by Judge Allen G. Buttrick, one of the defendants, a giant Malcolm L. Jarvis, shook the bars of the prisoner's cage in a frenzy and shouted, "Why don't you find me guilty of murder, and send me to the chair?"

"The people" concluded that this was, "A judicial determination of punishment, justly inflicted on convicted criminals." These "people" were not our people—as everyone could gather by the way "our people" responded to the sentence. Our people would have made more of an equitable decision—kinda like the one the judge made on the white girls' behalf.

The article continued:

> Three Girls Jailed: Given identical terms with Jarvis and Malcolm Little, of Dale Street, Roxbury, two of the girls, Beatrice Bazarian and her sister, Joyce Garagulian, both of Cambridge, were given five year terms in Sherborn, a woman's prison in Massachusetts, suspended. Kora Marderosian, of First Street, South Boston, was given a suspended sentence and placed on probation. All, pleaded guilty, to breaking and entering homes in Belmont, Arlington and Newton. Also, of looting them of furs and jewelry, valued at several thousands of dollars.

All of my Christian life, I questioned man's ability to make determinations about God. Those few months of intense prayer and searching for God while awaiting trial represented a major step for me, but after receiving an eight to ten year prison term, it made me wonder if I had prayed to the wrong God. Or maybe, if my court-appointed lawyer didn't handle our case like a "Peanuts" cartoon, we would have stood a chance.

After sentencing, we were sent to the state prison at Charlestown, Massachusetts. This old prison, built of huge granite blocks in the early 1700s, was certainly not the place to come if one were looking for even the slightest of creature comforts—like a water faucet. In fact, in time I would come to find my only comforts here were mental, not physical.

Often in my youth, I had heard stories of convicts and ex-convicts who would swear they were innocent—many behind bars "didn't do it." Well, to my horror and surprise, I found myself in prison for a two-week looting spree, which was encouraged by three white girls I really didn't even know.

My 6' × 12' cellblock was a damp, miserable, mouse and lice-infested excuse for living quarters. I lived out of a steel pitcher of warm water and a small wooden bucket for defecation. My living space was absolutely cramped. There was no running water in the cellblocks, and an undersized cot served as my bed. Yet, imprisonment—although it was definitely punishment—became a blessing in disguise, for me. Being locked up for 17 hours a day forced me to listen to my own thoughts, to listen to myself—not always an easy prospect for a youngster.

For the first few months of confinement, I was in such a state of mental shock, rebellion, fear and disbelief that I actually felt—and watched—my character and personality distort themselves. I had a lot of thinking to do yet. My mind slowly became unstable, confused and conflicted. Incarceration with no refuge was the problem. Outside, if I were either troubled by or bored with anything, all I had to do was to find some kind of distraction—and of those, there were plenty. Here, I was forced to confront myself, to work on myself, to face and to deal with my inner conflicts about the girls, my life and my choices. I was ill-equipped. Lying in the gloom of my damp cell, I found myself talking to myself. If a prison guard would have heard or have seen me, he would have reported it to the authorities. The authorities, in turn, would have thought me crazy, and would have had me committed to Bridgewater, yet another institution—only, for the criminally insane—especially since they had not yet forgotten my award-winning performance in court. It was at this time that I heard about the prison experiences of Jean Genet, the famous French playwright, who wrote *The Blacks*. It just so happened he'd produced an autobiography about these experiences called *The Thief's Journal*. The title of this book reminded me of Malcolm X. I wondered then, if it were really his journal they found, or if I was implicated in some other way—and what about the third man, Johnson? Why wasn't he in court?

On my cot, I was balanced between the razor-thin edges of sanity and insanity. As I said, that's when I was forced to look at my life critically. I was forced to come to grips with much that I, up to this time, had either denied or dismissed about myself. I saw myself for the first time as a willing scapegoat, suffering from the consequences of the negative actions of those with whom I had associated, and those self-fulfilled prophesies of an apathetic society. I realized that in every respect, all of my life, I had acted like a puppet whose strings were the wishes of others, and whose master was the devil himself. I saw how following the crowd while being intellectually unconscious and reveling in my own stupidity was the reason for my incarceration. As I existed outside the walls of my own mind, I was a caricature of the man I thought I was within my own mind.

Searching for a reason, a fundamental cause for my demise, my immediate conclusion was: "My religious beliefs were the main cause of my mental frustrations." Cop-out? Oversimplification? No, my mind was going through a metamorphosis, a transmutation of sorts. Up for grabs first were my most fundamental beliefs, my cornerstone of faith: my religion—the Supreme Power, or what people interpret to mean God, the "Holiest of Holies," a transcendent force about which I had heard and in which I had believed all of my life—all aspects of my fundamental beliefs came under bitter attack. The realization that I discovered

I'd been deceived by the religious beliefs I'd been taught all my life was just beginning to come forward at this time.

Daily, I found myself grappling with moral questions, such as: Is religion really the opiate of the people, the masses? If there is a God, then why, over 75 percent of the world, do people act as barbarously as if there isn't? Has the Global Village become our cave and these new atomic weapons, our club? Aren't all men mortal? Aren't we our brother's keepers? Then why is this man's inhumanity to me allowing him to build more of these institutions where he legally exacts slave labor and wages from me and others, rather than helping us to work through our problems?

In an attempt to satisfy my thirst for wisdom and knowledge, and to get to the root of my existential struggle, I began studying theology, etymology and ancient history. Slowly and surely I became a thinking, conscious person. I began questioning authority—especially that of my spiritual/religious leaders. I could not help projecting my resentment towards both them and towards the authority of those under whom I was serving my sentence. In fact, at that time either I saw all authority figures as wolves in sheep's clothing, leading the masses to their slaughter while throwing up smoke screens, or I saw their lack of genuine concern as just keeping us desensitized in an imaginary comfort zone, transistor radios in hand, while they built atomic bombs and experimented with nuclear energy capable of destroying all life on Earth. For example, why couldn't we work on the problem between the brothers of North and South Korea, rather than to give them a bomb to blow each other's brains out?

I explored religion's cultural reverberance within my own family. It was our symbolic "nose ring" which we accepted, without a fuss, believed unquestionably and inculcated almost as a reflex. There was no questioning, critical thinking, analysis, not the slightest active thinking or resistance. Yet, what if either the messenger or the message was flawed? How could we make up for the devastation across the generations? After all, was this the faith, the religion of my real fathers who traveled the savannas of Africa? I clearly saw how this habit of accepting prima facie evidence in my life had led to my downfall in that I never learned the practice of differentiation—or even more fundamental, I never learned to question authority. In learning about the supreme authority, it was bred into me that, that sort of authority goes unquestioned. Having met the "Honorable" Judge Buttrick and the district attorney made me shudder to think that if people like these had anything to do with the inculcation of knowledge—as they did the administration of justice—then their entire clientele would be doomed.

One of the interesting things I learned in studying the Bible is that it had an answer for just about everything. It taught me to do likewise. For example; the phrase "Beware, lest you be deceived" jumped out at me at this time. How apropos. I regret I never learned of these warnings earlier in life. I come from several generations of strong African American males. I'm sure somewhere along the lines in our genealogy, someone must have discovered the truth—yet, nobody told me. Why? Did they think I had to learn the hard way? Did they think my heart was hardened against reason? Don't get me wrong; I understand that occasionally people reject conventional wisdom and live by the dictates of their own minds and hearts. I witnessed this phenomenon in my son—a product of the 1960s. And when phenomena like this occur, people are very quick to look at the results without recognizing or owning up to their level of responsibility relative to its cause. For example, I could definitely see how this judge and district attorney could make even a mangy rat jump ship. Those men were dangerous, I thought.

In response to the judge: "A thinking person is a dangerous person"—especially to unscrupulous people both "within" and "without" positions of power. To people like that, thinking people become a threat, a menace to all of society. Often, thinking people are killed. Unfortunately, such was the case of the late Dr. Martin Luther King, Jr., the late Malcolm X and Gandhi (who was fatally shot by a Hindu fanatic in New Delhi).

Often, my higher thoughts were just at the sills of my consciousness, trying desperately to reveal themselves to me. Not understanding, I did what most people do. I forced myself to become distracted both with carnal desires—in the form of pornography (nudes and bikinis)—and, in particular, by engaging in stupid, meaningless conversations. I wanted to hear neither my heart nor its music from within. I remained in constant battle with my spiritual nature, as it kept knocking on both the doors of my heart and at the doorsills of my perception. One day, light dawned. I saw that I was running from the reality of my own nature—a most fundamental sign of the fear of self-discovery. I came to see that fear, ignorance and, ultimately, self-denial were at the root of my problems. The mental turmoil, anguish and total confusion persisted. I was fighting myself and in bitter denial of the fact that my mind, almost of its own accord, was changing fundamentally. I couldn't help noticing the fact that I desired, intensely, wisdom and knowledge—something which had not been in the vocabulary of my past experiences. I found I wanted to become the master of my own thoughts and actions and to spend time learning of myself, because not knowing why I was where I was, or how I got there, and knowing that I was going to be there for quite some time—and almost got a whole lot more "time" than that—I knew I had better come to grips with this force or aspect of myself which had kept me blind unto myself.

The metamorphosis which followed played itself out in strange ways. As I said earlier, I thought I was going crazy. For example, one day while I was doing my daily prison chores I remember my mind had gone off, perusing the stratosphere, without me. Exactly how this was made manifest, I don't know. What I do know is that I must have appeared very strange to those around me, because my mind was snapped back to Earth by the approach of another inmate.

"Who are you speaking to?" he asked me in a very gruff manner.

Angered by this intrusion, I snapped back, sarcastically, "Was I speaking to anyone?" I then painted my face with a sardonic smile.

"Well, your lips were moving, and you were looking dead at me like I did something to ya, or said something to ya," he conceded.

Outwardly, I played it off as a joke. Inwardly, I immediately became very concerned. I had not been incarcerated long, and already I was talking to myself. Having grown up thinking that a person who talks to themselves was crazy, I knew something within me was in the process of unraveling. I occupied myself by returning to my studies. My studies led me to believe that "understanding" would become a "master key" for me, and as a symbolic key, it would open many doors revealing to me who I was and what I was going through, both internally and externally. I came to find that through faith and belief, I could literally build up both a tolerance and a resistance to those external forces threatening my mental stability. I found that self-discovery was the gateway to understanding. It was the symbolic master key unlocking the door to the unknown realm of the human soul, ultimately leading to both Heaven and Paradise.

I found residing within the hallowed walls of my soul the Almighty Supreme Power, Creator, the All in All, "Everything Contained Within Everything." I began to see that the more introverted I had become, the wiser and the more aware I had become. I saw that Malcolm X's self-possession had sprung from this source also. He knew who he was and just what he was capable of; in other words, all aspects of his life, to him, were fully understood. There were no surprises. To others observing him yet being unaware of themselves, he was mesmerizing—and always full of surprises. I came to conclude that's why he was so grossly misunderstood by his public. In the past, I don't know how many times I felt it was a miracle I was not killed as a result of many of Malcolm's "pranks" (like the Dutch Shultz and the Johnny McGovain incidents), as I called them. But here, in prison, I'd come to a better understanding of myself and the world around me, and of the man who would later be called "Malcolm X."

As I was scanning these depths of personal understanding, I recall I wrote my mother at this time. I became so frustrated from being confined and disgusted that I wrote her a letter telling her some things that were far beyond the comprehension of a man as ignorant and stupid as I was supposed to be.

Of course, whenever I wrote home, I always wrote symbolically and philosophically. I purposely wrote this way because of the rigid censorship of the mail coming and going in prison. My mother and I had a mutual understanding. Of course, being my mother, she always seemed to understand just what I was thinking. The letter went like this:

> Dear Mother,
> Have you ever stopped to realize that in prison man's emotions become pent up within him, thus making him a frustrated individual? You know if you were to fill a balloon with water, and by some method force just one drop more into the balloon than its elasticity could bear, it would burst. Then the water would flow freely to wherever it would go. Well, it works likewise with the human body, only when my emotions break loose from me, I hope fate will make them flow into some constructive channels, not otherwise. All I can say now is I have been as close to death as one man can get without actually dying.
> At the present time, I have lost the fear of death—"He has no fear of any living thing or person upon the face of the earth." I would much rather be dead than to give these people another five years of my life. This is truly the way I feel, so I sincerely hope you and the family will get together and do what you can to free me from the clutches of these evil forces which have me imprisoned behind bars.
> Your Son,

The studies of religion I delved into were fantastic. They broadened my understanding. I studied Islam, Hinduism, Bhuddism, African religion and more. I questioned everything. Soon, I was able to begin formulating ideas about religion which came from my own head, not the heads of others. For example, in time, I came to see Jesus, Himself, as a man who passed through the forbidden door of knowledge and into the realms of the unknown—both in the "above," and in the "below." Jesus went, saw, felt, understood and taught the truths of the Heaven and the Hell, which is "within" and "without" each of us. And Jesus, like those we mentioned above, was both condemned and crucified for His teachings. Human nature has not changed much from classical antiquity to now—in all probability, these Techno/Nuclear Age Christians could be worse than their ancestors. For, in this Age of Enlightenment, in this Information Age, this age of technology, the ignorance of the few in power becomes the scourge—at pain of death— of the many who serve them. We don't need to look at the Ayatollah, Kadahfi or Saddam Hussein. Right here, in America, Bull Connor, J. Edgar Hoover and David Duke provide adequate examples of those deceivers of mankind who have used the teachings of a just and righteous man to enslave, to kill and to keep most of their loyal followers wallowing in a totality of ignorance—and surprisingly, many of these conflicted individuals, unable to live within their own reality, often seek a charismatic movement or leader for "purpose." Yet, when dealing with minorities, my experience is, they substitute a superiority complex for an inferiority complex. They conceal it in their impressions and expressions of the actions and events pertaining to others— the worst of the three being J. Edgar Hoover. And what's more frightening about many of these people, like Senator Joseph McCarthy, is that they rise usually to the highest levels of government and leadership.

On the contrary, I came to learn that in nature, the source of all Earth's creations is infinite, and is enshrouded in an atmosphere of tranquillity and eternity. Peace lies at the end of the road for the man or woman who would take the time to learn of the God within themselves. Those who have exercised this knowledge have presented the world with great, beautiful treasures of art, music and science of matchless quality. They have followed their hearts, their minds, their imaginations and have reaped the full benefits of their self-discipline. They have been able to break away from their old physical and mental "habits of mind, spirit and body," from Einstein and the Dali Lama, to artists of all kinds.

Upon reading about these endeavors, and experiencing something similar happening to me, whereas I had earlier been terrified of it, I now got very excited about this process. But the demands of this ascetic walk—purification, intense self-discipline, the courage to walk an uncharted path through the regions of my mind, enduring intense mental conflict in pursuit of purity of thought, of life, and of character—was so big to me, it was of heroic proportions.

Having discovered this way of life and having decided to work on it, my first inclination was to tell others, and through the telling, to justify chastising them without putting myself in their place—to get a better glimpse of their point of view. Judging my fledgling flock of listeners, how much different was I from the judge and the district attorney who sentenced me? Wasn't I sentencing these inmates who, it seems, didn't have a clue as to what I was talking about; individuals, who, for all I know, might really have thought I was a bonefide fruitcake? Again, from the Bible: "Let he who is without sin cast the first stone."

The way was teaching me of the importance of humility. I had to become perfectly clear about my own understanding of this process before I could presume to tell anyone else how to be "right in the world"—also, bear in mind, my pulpit was my cell block. I was the oppressed, in process of becoming the oppressor, dampening the souls and spirits of my would-be followers like a cold ocean fog, displacing their own peace of mind, faith and, ultimately, their motivation, "giving them a shoeshine"—and they were wearing sandals. Criticism had brought me to the point of humility. It taught me how ignorant of the laws of life I was. Didn't I learn that between cosmos and chaos, between Heaven and Hell, between time and space, between the infinite, the nonextant and the eternal, there existed worlds and dimensions of possibility? And a human, being created in the likeness of God, held within them all of those infinite possibilities? Humility had shed upon me the light of understanding.

The incarceration of Malcolm X and me had brought about in me a psychological metamorphosis. Ultimately, being forced to be still and to ponder the way I had lived my life on the streets, I arrived at a much deeper level of self-awareness. My decision to follow my thoughts and to pursue a higher level of understanding was the key, igniting the mental transmutation I was blessed to have experienced. With all my thoughts and disillusionment concerning Christianity, it is a wonder I was not transformed into a Faustus, of sorts. On the contrary, I thank

God for helping me through this period by allowing me the mental capacity to help myself—for, like the moral to my grandfather's story of the pigeon in the chicken coop says, if I were content not to venture into the far recesses of my own mind, I would have been content not to have made the huge gains which had—and continue to have—transformed me. Nothing ventured, nothing gained—pure and simple.

5
Transgression—of the Mind

FREEDOM IS A STATE OF MIND,
NOT A PHYSICAL CONDITION.

We cannot be free or know freedom while being arbitrarily dominated, ruled under the idiosyncrasies and perversities of an instituionally-grown monolithic entity like Colonialism or Imperialism.
The mental shock alone would deteriorate the emotional vibrancy of our intellect.
Suffering from this delusionary behavior would make us quiet and withdrawn.
Although our fear would be the beginning of our ultimate introduction to real knowledge, and knowing something is better than knowing nothing, yet, some people would prefer dancing with wolves, to walking the path of knowlege. This level of righteousness is nearly impossible to teach people who think they know everything and who, in reality, know nothing. As the Persian poet instructs us, we must learn wisdom like the pupil of the eye which looks upon all things, yet is blind unto itself, and (in size) is more humble than most it sees.
A person who stands united with their thoughts conceives magnificently of others first, and then upon reflection, themselves. The good—or evil—that is seen reflects their own good—and evil. The qualities of their mind are magnified in their acquaintances, and every emotion of their heart, in someone. People cleave to one person and avoid others (according to their own likeness—or unlikeness—of themselves) truly seeking themselves in their associates. The manifestations of these mental projections are evident in their work, their habits and their gestures. Nobody has ever indulged in an over-inflated sense of pride, which wasn't injurious to

themselves. A person cannot do wrong without suffering wrong for so doing. One way or another, we all reap what we sow in this world.

An alternative to all that is, "transgression."

The key to mind transgression is self-containment.

—By Malcolm "Shorty" Jarvis

I would like to preface this chapter with an explanation of why I wrote it. In my time, I have seen those who delve into matters of the mind—the most powerful tool with which a human being has to work—brandished as incompetents, from Sigmund Freud to the local "witch-doctor." It is almost as if western medicine knows all too well the powers of the mind, and how one's mind "at ease" can heal, and "in dis-ease" can kill; the power lies within the individual. Just imagine what would happen to skyrocketing medical costs if people began healing themselves using their minds—not to mention the penchant for cottage industries bursting at the seams with "home remedies"? It is almost as if, in western culture, there's an economic reason for keeping people at the troughs of ignorance concerning the powers of their own minds. I believe we have an unhealthy disassociation with anything that concerns the mind.

The now exiled Tibetan Dali Lama was recently on a tour of the United States. At a press interview on April 24, 1997, he made a statement which has rung in my ears since. It went something like this: "America spends much time, effort and money on outer space, and precious little time, money, energy or concern on inner space."

I remember thinking to myself, "The Dali Lama is on to something." I hope we are able to hear it. That was the first time I'd heard anyone mention anything about the workings of western civilization as they affect the masses and their search for spirituality as truth from within ourselves—within our minds. Again, it is as if this subject matter is so seldom discussed publicly for fear of total ridicule. It is frowned upon, generally. It is almost as if we, as a culture, suffer from a spiritual phobia. Yet, in more "primitive" societies there is not only a place for this kind of activity, but there is also a person who, serving as spiritual guide and leader, facilitates the process—the shaman, the witch doctor, the voodoo priest, the medicine man, etc. (In western culture on the other hand, even the names we accord these professionals are often degrading or in some way, jaded—further, many of these "primitive" practitioners hold flame throwers to western culture's matchbook of psychotherapy.)

The title of this chapter is, "Transgression—of the mind." It's ironic that I speak in terms of something which is so beneficial to the mind, body and soul with terms we use to describe a violation or, more commonly, a sin. Here, the Dali Lama's words ring ominously true. Unfortunately, it is a transgression of sorts for us to delve into our own minds to sort out our existence and to set ourselves onto a path of healing and well-being. On an individual basis, it is important we ask ourselves, "Why?"

I use the word "transgression" to indicate a "crossing over," from the conscious to the subconscious mind, because that is basically what happened to Malcolm X and me. Not only did our introverted sides take over—being the extroverts we were—but also, externally, we had lost all of our former distractions without the chance to reconcile anything with anyone. For my part, guilt tormented me. My mind was all over the place. I knew if I didn't control my mind, somehow I would either go crazy or be considered mentally unstable. I needed a distraction of some sort, or I needed to pursue, to follow these feelings, to stay within touch of them and what they were causing my mind to do.

This "transgression" was little more than a daydream, which I followed consciously into my subconscious mind. It is like a painter or sculptor who goes into a trance while watching a blank wall or a tree trunk as he waits for either a spiritual inspiration, enlightening or (more simply stated) for the wall or bole to tell him what to paint or to sculpt. Using this process of "transgressing" beyond self-imposed limits makes it possible to reach a higher level of experiencing life. Anyone involved in thinking on a profound cerebral scale—especially in the arts (sculptors, musicians, writers, etc.)—"transgresses" or crosses over into their subconscious minds often. It is a natural process. It is also a spiritually cleansing process. Many are just not aware of it and how beneficial it can be. What I am describing here is nothing new, but the term I have chosen to describe the process might be new to some. I just trust you bear with me.

I do not consider myself one of the great thinkers of the western world. I am no Freud—nor would I want to be treated like him. But, of all the western thinkers who've pondered the inner workings of and the issues surrounding discoveries within the mind, the one who comes closest to describing "transgression" is that bold and daring thinker, Sigmund Freud. Freud understood that all parts of the mind coexist as equally important and that dreams—aside from being an avenue whereby we can witness more clearly our own past, present and future realities by paying closer attention to signs on the dreamscape which we might have thought meaningless—are a superhighway to the subconscious mind.

Going against the rigidly ordered view of the mind prevalent in the 19th century, Freud, although considered brilliant, was also considered by some a reckless thinker. Freud was a dreamer. And for Freud, ultimately, dreams could assist tremendously in the process, the search of self-discovery and self-direction.

The process of, and the sensory impression during, a "mental transgression" is quite similar to a dream. For me, it was a dream in which I was a participant. (Engaging this process transferred into my everyday, conscious life any "good" I derived by being in this state. It worked with a residual effect, eventually cleansing me.) After hurdling the many emotional barriers of my past extroverted life, and then passing through several additional stages, I arrived at a state of relative purity. It was quite an emotional gauntlet, as you will see. Again, "primitive" societies by and large are leaps and bounds ahead of most western practitioners in this area. For example: in Australia, the aborigines have an experience, a state they call "Dream-time." Dream-time is similar to what Haitians attribute to either the walking dead's zombie life or a voodoo "possession." It speaks of a process whereby time and the reality of life as we know it are suspended. (And not only their reality, but also their sensory perceptions undergo a change. For example, zombies have been known to have spikes driven through their bodies without either feeling pain or bleeding. And during the Rite of Kanzo, a voodoo priest's body is "mounted" or possessed by the particular god-spirit which acts through the person who speaks in tongues and acts like the god possessing them at the time—Damballah, Ogun, etc. During this ceremony, the priest not only walks on fire for extended periods of time, but also holds it in both hands without getting burned.)

Suffice to say, the mind is more powerful than I can explain. I simply ask that you indulge me, that you bear with me in this chapter. In order to accept this idea of "mind transgression," you will have to be open, pure-intentioned and well-disciplined in your approach to gain understanding of such an activity. What I will describe to you are the stages, the gauntlet through which I passed before experiencing a "transgression."

It was not until after my imprisonment that I really began to find myself. My prison sentence was eight to ten years. That meant, according to state law, I was to serve 64 months (five years and four months) before I would be eligible for parole. I awaited trial for two months in the county jail. During that time I was mentally building myself up for an awful letdown again. I didn't expect to receive more than a couple of years at the most for the crime I had committed against society. The heavy sentence I did receive came as a terrific shock to me. It seemed all my self-directed inner fears, combined with the fear of going to prison, broke loose from me, returned, and struck me square in the face.

As I mentioned before, I believe I lost my mind when the judge passed sentence on me. Again, I was told later that I caused a bad scene by screaming at the judge. At that time it seemed the screaming was the only thing I do remember. I don't recall what I said, in total. It appeared my mind was a complete blank after that. I also remember feeling like I was in a dream state. I refused to let myself believe or face the reality of being sent to prison. When darkness finally cleared away from my brain, the next thing I realized was that I was sitting in the gloom of a damp miserable state prison cellblock.

The prison colony was not operated in the same way most prisons are operated throughout the country. The prison colony was an institution for the criminal who had some redemptive qualities. It was considered a place of correction. In other words, an inmate in a correctional institution had hopes of some day returning to society as a good, rehabilitated citizen.

The colony was composed of two farm units outside the 33-foot high wall, and had inmates who were considered honest and trustworthy. Outside the wall was a farm-like expanse in the deep country. Most of the farm inmates had only a few months of their time to go, so it would be real stupid of them to try to escape with so little time left to go before their day of freedom arrived.

By the same token, there was a "dungeon." The dungeon was what prisoners called the cell block or solitary confinement, where an inmate would sleep on nothing but a large slab of stainless steel. In some of the older prisons, the slab was made of hard wood, which would make it more bearable, but not here. Time in solitary confinement would always be spent in complete darkness. To my knowledge, there were no mice in that area. But, there were plenty of lice, and each night the inmate was served up as the honored guest at their dinner table. Needless to say, brushing off these lice all night did not permit an inmate to get a good night's sleep.

Again, there were no toilet facilities in the block except a wooden bucket in each cell, all of which had contained such violent odors, they alone could turn a man deathly sick with every attempt to use one. The 12 units inside the prison colony had 50 men to each, and one house officer.

One of the biggest and most important jobs of the prison colony administration was to investigate its inmates to understand them and determine effective rehabilitation programs and procedures. In other words, the institution wanted to know what made an inmate tick—what were his ways of thinking and the reasons for it. To that end, they opened and read all of the mail and often made carbon copies of such for their records. In many respects, inmates had no rights. So, for example, if I were to be caught doing anything untoward, they'd have "eaten me for lunch" without being held accountable to anyone.

During the first few months of my confinement, I uncomfortably watched and felt my character and personality distorting themselves away from the self-delusionary lies which I had been feeding myself all my life. I began to realize then that I had been running from those inner feelings of truth all my life. I felt like Zorba the Greek, ball and chained in Singapore. Now that I was confined to a cell, there was no place for me to run and seek refuge, and certainly no one to talk to. Therefore, I was forced to face and to deal with my inner conflicts. This is where my trip into the realms of the unknown really began.

How strange—this was the year (1946) Mother Frances X. Cabrini was canonized, becoming the first U.S. saint in the Catholic Church. It's almost as if there was a dominating spirituality in the air, for this was also the year Malcolm X and I would discover our "Transgression of the Mind" theory. The following year (1947) they would find the now famous "Dead Sea Scrolls." Astrologically, something profound was happening.

One night, while lying on my prison cot, staring up at the granite ceiling of my cell, the battle of "myself and I" began. I started asking myself impertinent questions, which I would argue with myself about, but couldn't answer to my own satisfaction. Mind you, I came from a very religious family, and I now came to the conclusion that it was many of my religious beliefs that were the cause of most of my mental conflicts.

Please understand, I blame myself for being so stupid as to wind up in prison. I made a pact that I would not leave prison as ignorant as

I had entered. But, in truth, a good deal of my thinking had been done for me by other people, and I had gotten myself into the habit of believing in and relying on the opinions of others. (In fact, to this day, I believe anyone who wholeheartedly swallows popular conceptions and general opinions is letting others do their thinking for them.)

If you can imagine in your own mind the picture as it was (night after night, day after day, I was asking myself a million times, "Why? Why? Why am I in prison?") then you will glimpse an idea of what I am talking about.

One night, while asking myself this question, a voice spoke to me from out of the atmosphere of my gloomy, damp cell and said, "Listen, my son. Listen to me."

At first I thought I was going crazy. There was nobody in my cell. But who could have spoken to me? I got up from my cot and walked around the small space I had, trying to convince myself that it was pure imagination. Inwardly, or should I say, subconsciously, I knew that it wasn't. I looked through the bars of my cell to assure myself there was no one around trying to play a joke on me or anything like that. I knew the prison guard had made his hourly check ten minutes prior, and was not due back for another 40 minutes.

Then it happened again. I could feel it all around me. It was a feeling I had never felt before in all my life. The voice seemed to speak again, saying, "My son, my son, trouble not yourself, but lie down on your bed and relax. Listen to me and I will tell you all your heart's desires."

Being a little confused, I went back to bed. I had no sooner relaxed when the words of my mother came back to me. I recalled how she taught me when I was a child to listen always to the voice of God whenever He spoke to me. He would guide and keep me all the days of my life. Then I started to wonder to myself, "Could this be the voice of the true God speaking to me? Is this what the other side is like—Heaven being eternal peace, and Hell being eternal, guilt-driven torment?

If it was the voice of God, perhaps He was trying to communicate to me just how near he was to me. At that moment, the voice spoke again, and this time, I knew it was neither my imagination nor the "Big Sleep."

"If I talk to this voice, perhaps I can learn something nobody else knows," I thought to myself.

I listened for another moment. It seemed to be whispering in my ear, "My son, I know your heart's desires and will tell you your very thoughts."

I thought to myself, "Now who or what could know me well enough to tell me my heart's desires and my very own thoughts?"

I was about to debate this thought with myself when the voice started whispering in my ear again. "My son," it seemed to say, "Why do you doubt yourself? Why do you fight within yourself? Don't you know you are doing these things against your own will and against yourself? By so doing you become your own worst enemy. Just lie still and listen to me. You, my son, have come from a very nice family. You are not as bad as some people are inclined to believe. This I know."

I then interrupted the voice by thinking a question. Before the thought was completed, I was listening to the answer. The question was, "Why am I in prison?" The answer was, "You are in prison because it is the will of your Supreme Being."

I thought to myself, "But I don't understand. What internal or external power would will a man to prison? Please, if you will, tell me why."

The voice, answering, said, "Many years ago, while you were a child, you used to pray to me every night. You asked of me many things in those days, things that were given to you. Today, you seemed to have forgotten I exist. As long as you were at liberty, indulging yourself in the lusts of the earth and polluting your soul with the evils of the devil, you were the phony, 'big-shot' you thought yourself to be. In the meantime, you were descending into the bottomless pits of Hell."

I interrupted the voice and asked in a soft voice, "Who are you?"

It answered in a nonchalant manner, "My real name has been kept from you for many years. When the time comes, it will come to you. I am He who has been with you from birth, and with your mother and father and their mother and father before them. I am what you might call your soul, your spirit or your subconscious mind—whichever is your choosing."

"I wish to call you my soul," I said, "because I can feel you even though I can't see you. You feel like a patient and loving big brother directing me unto paths of righteousness. But I shall forever be searching to find out your true name. Please tell me, oh soul of mine, will you tell me the million things I would like to know?" (I was so glad my soul was kind to me. It could have—like they did in the Tokyo Tribunal to their "War Heroes"—sentenced me to eternal death and damnation.)

"I'm sorry," my soul said, "but I'll tell you what I will do. I won't tell you a million things, but I will grant you three of your heart's desires.

If you choose very wisely from the many desires you have, I promise, you will be able to satisfy your other curiosities. Tell me now, my son, what are the three foremost desires of your heart?"

I answered, "Oh, my soul, I would not be behind prison bars if I were a wise man. Therefore, my first desire in life is to obtain understanding and to exercise wisdom. I realize if I knew a little bit about a lot of things I would have known enough about the law to have kept myself out of prison. Therefore, my second desire in life is to learn of knowledge. Now, I know if I could see as far as you, into the realms of the unknown and, like you, could understand what I saw, I would then know exactly why I am in prison. So my third and last desire in life is to have my common sense restored. I honestly do believe, oh soul of mine, if you were to grant me these three wishes, the final outcome would lead to my existence in a state of perfection."

"My son, my son. You don't know how happy I am to see that you have selected so wisely. I will now give you three rules to guide you along the path of righteousness. There will be one rule for each of your desires.

> **Rule One:** Remember at all times, that you don't know anything and you can always learn something. This rule is the foundation of all wisdom.
> **Rule Two:** Study very hard and study many subjects. Always know a little something about a lot of things. This is the key to the doors of knowledge and understanding.
> **Rule Three:** Abide by the Ten Commandments of the Holy Scriptures and you will obtain wisdom, understanding and experience a restoration of your common sense.

"I am very sorry my son, but I must now take leave of you. Do as I have instructed you, and remember, above all, THE KEY TO ALL SUCCESS LIES WITHIN YOUR OWN SOUL."

The voice then faded away. As I lay on my cot staring at the black steel bars of my gloomy cell, I wondered to myself if this had all been a trick of the mind, a nightmare, or if this voice was going to be my guiding light through this dark and frightening prison experience. I knew it couldn't have been a dream or anything like that. I was wide awake and the conversation had left too vivid an impression on my mind. It made too much sense to be folly. I don't recall exactly when I went to sleep that night, but I don't think I got more than a couple of hours rest.

For the next few weeks, all I did was think about all the things that had been told to me that night. One day, not long after this experience, I spoke with Malcolm X about this event. I came to find that he had experienced something similar, too. After much animated discussion, we decided to name this experience, and to study and to analyze it in an attempt to fully understand it. We came up with the conclusion that the only term we could use to describe these most remarkable events which happened to both of us around the same time was "transgression." It was a literal interpretation of our mutual experiences, as we had agreed our conscious minds had "crossed over" into that of our subconscious.

But relative to dissecting and understanding it, naming it was child's play. For weeks, I lay each night figuratively tossing and turning in hopes of figuring out what was happening to me. This self-communication, although popular today, was not kosher in the 1940s, and if anyone caught me and inquired about what was going on, I had better come up with a good excuse, otherwise I'd be declared mentally incompetent, and that would have been "it" for me. In those days, treatment of the mentally disturbed was brutal. Aside from summarily being sterilized, they were also often abused. Nevertheless, now that I knew how to "transgress," I had been engaging in it quite regularly. As a result, I had put myself under pressure.

I was still unsure of all that was happening to me. I knew simply that something new, different, strange and wonderful was going on. Of what it was, I was as yet unaware. I knew simply that I'd developed beautiful "voices in my mind," capable of producing anything I wished—from thoughts to beautiful music. For example, one afternoon while playing the prison piano, I accidentally struck a series of chord progressions which suddenly cast a spell over me. I felt as though I was dreaming. In reality, though, I was wide awake. This series of chords seemed to blend with the flowing of my blood through my veins. I felt a thrill that ran from my head to my feet and back again. I knew this was really something out of the ordinary, so I wrote the chords down on a piece of music manuscript paper and played them over and over again.

After a short while, I imagined I heard a beautiful melody which blended with these chords like water meets water. After an hour or so of being in another world, I realized I had composed my first song and all of its beautiful melody. Finally I thought I would let someone else play this strange, mystifying music. I would watch and listen to see if I could discover any more about the mysterious sphere from whence this music came.

Days later, I attended a rehearsal of the prison orchestra and asked the music director (who happened to be an accomplished pianist) to play this music for me. Until now, I'd considered it a "straw harp." Yet, as he played it, I carefully observed his eyes and facial expressions. No sooner had he struck the first chord than I knew he had been cast into a mysterious frame of mind—the same as I. Upon finishing the music, he just sat still while staring into space, deep in contemplation with a faraway look in his eyes.

Finally he spoke hazily and said, "This isn't an ordinary piece of music. It is something much more than that. It's so beautiful and it expresses so many feelings. It has so many living qualities. I wouldn't kill these fine qualities by making this a cheap ballad. In my opinion," he continued, "it's got one of those melodies that would make a masterpiece if it were properly developed."

I was surprised to hear him say this. I knew he understood the feelings that lay beneath the foundation of this music. I could hear it in his interpretative playing. This was all well and good. The only incomprehensible thing was the fact that I was not a pianist and knew practically nothing about playing piano. I possessed only a rudimentary working knowledge of the piano keyboard from my past studies of harmony and counterpoint.

To this day, whenever I am so mentally preoccupied as to lapse into a trance or daydream, I find that I can actually feel creations in their embryonic stage shaping themselves into something greater within me. However slow I work out these ideas, I'm always amazed at the fact that these ideas are generated and sometimes take on a shape of their own, aligning themselves with the organic matter of the material world. I find that very often this happens with me when conditions are profoundly silent. Then and only then can I reap the full benefits of the experience.

A different kind of soul experience occurred one hot summer night while I was lying on my stiff cot, staring up at the thick black bars of my gloomy prison cell. My mind commenced to playing tricks on me. Within me, this battle, this conflict of mind over matter, was raging profoundly. My mind was racing like a rocket. The more I thought, the more confused I became. Then I remembered what the voice of my soul had told me a few months before: to relax and many things would come to me, "The Key Lies Within Your Own Soul." So I decided to have a conversation with my own soul. I asked it to reveal to me the dynamics of the process in which we were engaging. My soul did not fail me.

I stopped twisting and turning and let my head sink into the soft pillow while my body became limp from relaxation. I was very groggy from a loss of sleep, yet I was half awake from vigorous thought when the soft voice again began to whisper in my ear. It said, "My son, my son, why do you trouble yourself?"

In no time, I was carrying on a conversation with myself again. The following dialogue took place between myself and I:

Myself: You know, my son, you will cause yourself to have a nervous breakdown if you don't take it easy.

I: I realize this, but I can't help it. I am thirsting for knowledge of the many things I would like to know.

Myself: Well, since you have tried very hard to follow my past instructions, perhaps I can help you again, now. But you must promise to use your knowledge only for constructive purposes. By this I mean, you should help others learn how to live clean, healthy lives, and how to respect one another as human beings regardless of race, creed or color.

I: Yes, I will try to do as I am instructed, but this is a tremendous task. People are so selfish and egotistical. How can I, as one person, change the world's way of thinking and doing things?

Myself: You can do it by having the same trust and faith in your fellow man as you have in yourself. I feel confident, with the whip of truth, you can do wonders to affect the peoples of the world by convincing them to see the need to go to their knees, if only you will give it a try.

I: Well, I will do what I can, but I will not succeed without your help.

Myself: I am indeed happy to see that you realize that you need help. You are getting wiser, everyday. You see, you cannot accomplish anything worthwhile without me, and I cannot do likewise without you. We need each other, implicitly.

I: One of the many things I am wondering about is the power of suggestion, and how the devil's scheme affects the human mind.

Myself: Let me give you an example; as long as the black people sleep in their shallow graves of ignorance, their extent of knowledge is going to remain far below that of 33 degrees—its rightful place. A motto of my adversary, Satan, is to divide and to conquer. This problem also applies to people. The black man is scattered into every nation on the face of the earth. But what is more interesting is what has been divided in the black community in order to conquer the black race—like family, skin-based pecking orders, college house and high school yard status, etc.—from slavery to today. This was all a part of the devil's horrible scheme.

I: How did the devil dupe the black people in order to dull their minds and to slow their ways of thinking down to nothing?

I suppose I must have fallen asleep at this point because I knew nothing until the next morning when I was awakened by a loud bell. This morning bell meant rise and shine, get washed and dressed, be seated at the breakfast table and ready to eat in one half hour.

The next night I began reading the Bible again. Strange as it may sound, I opened the Bible at random and started to read John 2:15–17. It read as follows: "Love not the world, neither the things that are in the world. If any man love the world, the love of the Father is not in him. For all that is in the world, the lust of the flesh and the lust of the eyes, and the pride of life, is not of the Father but is of the world. "And the world passeth away, and the lust thereof. He that doeth the will of God, abideth forever."

As I finished reading this last passage, I could feel a cool summer night's breeze which seemed to flow through the large prison window. This cold breeze slipped across my half-naked body as I lay on my cot with the Bible lying on my chest. I was very relaxed. I imagine I must have been meditating upon the truth I had just finished reading when I fell asleep and started dreaming. I dreamt about the ranch home I eventually bought, my family, all manner of things—interestingly enough, most of those things (like my ranch home) which I can remember dreaming about, in some way, became a part of my life in the real world.

Upon waking the next morning, I felt very peculiar. The dream had left a very deep impression on my mind. Since the prison inmates didn't have to work in the prison shops on Sundays, I had a full day to meditate upon the things on my mind in the solitude of my cell. At that moment, I was so obsessed with my thoughts that the ringing of the breakfast bells plagued me. Realizing I had to eat in order to live, I forced myself to "down" what little food I could. Remembering the instructions from my soul, I tried to relax and to let my mind dwell upon whatever it desired. Once again, it seemed as though I was talking to myself, mumbling my thoughts in a soft voice.

My mind wandered to the subject of food. I was thinking about how the food and meat we eat determines the quality of our bodies and the blood that flows through them. I thought also about whether or not the quality of our blood, when it flows through our brains, determines the quality of the mechanical and chemical functioning of those brain parts used in the forming of our thoughts and ideas. Well, at this time Malcolm and I were studying the new idea called trichinosis. It said basically, any underpurified meat that came from any part of a pig or bear that contained a small parasitic worm called a trichina worm was very dangerous. This worm infested the intestines of its host, and its larvae moved through the host's bloodstream, encysting themselves in the animal's muscle tissue carrying with them a disease, a condition called trichinosis. Trichinosis affected those who ate this undercooked meat. The problem was that the encysted larvae continued to survive in the new host's body. They matured in the intestines of their host and deposited their larvae in the intestinal wall of their host. When the larvae matured, they soon penetrated this wall and moved to other parts of the host body through the blood and lymphatic systems. They would also invade skeletal muscles and ultimately penetrate the brain and heart, often killing their host in the process. If you ask me, pretty serious consequences for eating a couple pork chops at a barbecue.

(Before the public read about trichinosis in the media of the sixties, Malcolm X and I had done our research—I am still amazed at the subjects we delved into while in prison. In fact, recently, I decided to check with *Mosby's Medical and Nursing Dictionary* (1986, pg. 1148) and Bernhard Grzimek's *Encyclopedia of Mammals*, Volume 3 (1990, pg. 21), to verify some of this data. It's amazing how the truth will continue to set you free over time.)

My musings continued: as many people know, alcohol is an intoxicant which is capable of causing physical and mental imbalance. There is no need to mention, in detail, what alcohol is capable of doing as most people know; many people have died because of it. Just imagine, if we were to have trichinosis, alcohol, and nicotine in our systems together what we would have in us. It is a miracle some of us are not dead—although we're now not physically dead, rest assured we are, mentally. If we do not realize what we have been doing to ourselves, we are our own worst enemy. We inflict harm upon ourselves, not realizing what we are doing. A person is what he eats. If one eats unclean swine? You go figure.

At this point, my mind seemed to drift back to a section of the Bible I had read some time ago. It had something to do with the pig. Reaching for the Bible, I opened it to Leviticus (11:3). The following is what I read: "Whatsoever parteth the hoof and is cloven hoofed, and cheweth the cud, among the beast, that shall ye eat." I thought to myself, this verse refers to animals like the cow, sheep, and deer. I read further: "Nevertheless, these shall you not eat of them that chew the cud or them that divide the hoof; as the camel, because he cheweth the cud, but divideth not the hoof; he is unclean unto you." And in 11:7: "And the swine, though he divideth the hoof, and be cloven footed, yet he cheweth not the cud; he is unclean to you." From Isaiah 66:17: "They that sanctify themselves, and purify themselves in the garden behind one tree in the midst, eating swine's flesh and the abomination, and the mouse, shall be soon consumed together, saith the Lord."

I let the Bible slide onto the top of my chest and started to reminisce about the pig—something I read in *Webster's Unabridged Dictionary* while studying etymology (and something which I have since checked with Grzimek's *Encyclopedia of Mammals*). I remember discovering some remote connection between the pig and the rat. I found that although most rodents are fairly small, in South America, there exists a giant water hog which is a rat in reality, but if it were in a pig pen, the butcher would never know the difference, it bears just such a resemblance to a domestic pig. I did not go any further with this research—but could you imagine?

This rudimentary research shook me with pain and disgust. We black and minority races of people live in shallow graves of ignorance and are kept enslaved mentally and physically (while being socially oppressed), I thought. We are so paralyzed by our daily struggle to survive that we don't have the time to do the kinds of research we need to survive. What a paradox. (Yet, had I not been incarcerated and later retired, I would not have been conducting research into the phylums, class, order and family of rodents and pigs.)

It is time the ruling class knew (and ancient history will bear this out) that while their Caucasian ancestors were living like animals in the caves of Europe, black people were living in a highly civilized world in the Near East. The white man, with all his degrees of knowledge, will never ever equal or duplicate the marvels of the world that black people have conceived and built—the Pyramids are but one of these marvels yet existing in the continent of the black man. Yet, self-destructive as it may be, today we persist in calling each other "Niggers," and thereby continue the work of the man who would enslave and define us—the man who would not allow us to speak our own native languages as slaves, who would lynch, shoot, and otherwise torture us if they caught us violating their arbitrary, controlling rules, who would cause many slaves to brood, grieve and finally die of sorrow. Such sorrows laid the groundwork for the Negro's famous spirituals, which, in addition to providing solace, provided Negroes at that time their only way of communicating.

According to Webster's dictionary, the word Negro comes from the Latin and Spanish word "niger," which means "black." It also says, "A Negro is a member of the typical African branch of the Ethiopian race." As far back as I could trace, use of the word Negro started in the year 1555 A.D. The white slavemaster first used this word when he brought the first blacks to this country to work for nothing, as both indentured servants and slaves. (No wonder the white man is so wealthy and controls the vast majority of the country's economy.) The first slaves did not come to this country in the year 1608 as U.S. history books would have people to believe.

According to *Funk & Wagnalls Standard College Dictionary*, it claims the word "Nigger" is: "A Negro or member of any dark-skinned people; a vulgar and offensive term." This is how most people think of minority and black people. But, as I understand it and see, there are a lot of white people to whom the term "Nigger" would fit a lot better than it would fit me or any other black person.

Another very important point is that an albino is considered somewhat unusual because he lacks pigmentation, thus making him white. The dictionary defines it thusly: "An abnormal condition in human beings characterized by a genetically-determined lack of pigmentation in certain cells of the skin, hair and eyes, giving a very white or pale appearance. Or, any organism lacking normal pigmentation."

I wondered what this statement made of white people, if original man was black? While pondering the answer to that question, my mind drifted to the subject of motion pictures, reading material and the part they play in this horrible scheme of keeping the masses ignorant. I was thinking of how pictures on television and in certain reading materials have tricked so many Negroes into damnation that the world will never know. What a shrewd but cunning operator Satan is. He knows that the human mind controls and plays tricks upon the human body. The power of suggestion is a part and parcel of this trick. Everything ever seen by the human eye registers upon the brain both consciously and subconsciously. Scientists have found that everything a person has seen during his lifetime is registered somewhere in his subconscious mind.

We may not realize it, but the subconscious mind is always influencing the conscious mind during our daily activities. There is not a day which goes by that we do not find ourselves doing one little act or another, instinctively. Satan, knowing many of these things, uses them to his advantage. The minority races of people are the victims and don't realize it, generally, until it is too late.

Many Negroes read the daily newspapers, magazines and see motion pictures, a vast majority of which are made by white men. One of the first things these men do, as mentioned before, is to show their woman scantily clad in bathing suits while offering up sexy poses. It is a natural thing for a man, when he sees a beautiful picture, to admire it; but in the case of "soft" pornography, after admiring it just so long, that admiration turns to lust. The Bible tells us, "If a man lusts after a woman in his heart, then he has already committed adultery with her." How many Negro and minority men have fallen into this ingenious trap of Satan? I speak about the Negro man because the percentage of Negro women fooled by Satan is relatively small—so small it is not worth mentioning.

In the final analysis, it is really the men who are doing most of the damage to the Negro race. I know. I saw it in the prisons then and I see it in the prisons today. "Black men prefer blondes," too, I know—I was one of those destructive Negro men. As long as Satan can keep the black man's mind between a white woman's legs, he will lead him and many of the Negro race straight to the bottomless pits of hell, like a cow on its way to the slaughter led by the ring in its nose.

Madison Avenue, by giving white females all sorts of superficial publicity, combined with superficial glamour, tricks the Negro man into believing that white women are superior to Negro women primarily because of their whiteness of skin. The Negro man in his effort to satisfy his ego and vanity goes lusting after what he already has within his own race of people. This is what people mean when they say, "A man can't see for looking." I have personally been a victim of this trap and scheme. But, through the mercy of Allah, I was fortunate not to get hooked as deeply as others. I find it almost an impossibility to list all the different ways Satan tempts people. His biggest trap is to trick his victims mentally. As long as black people are constantly occupied mentally and physically by material objects and the lust of the flesh, they will remain in Hell with Satan. Plain common sense should tell black people that they are the object of the devil's greatest exploits.

I arrived at the conclusion that as long as black people look toward external things in life, they will remain mentally dead. When they learn to look towards internal things for life and happiness, they will experience eternal peace while opening the door to the realms of the unknown.

As I stopped thinking for a moment, I glanced through the thick black bars of my prison cell. I caught a glimpse of the blue sky outside, and watched various formations of clouds moving in. To myself I wondered about some of the marvels of nature and asked myself why I never found time, while at liberty, to appreciate the sky, the mighty sea, the willow branches, the essence of life itself.

Then my mind drifted back to this racial problem, and its attendant conflicts. I went back to my cot seeking relaxation. I started questioning myself again. It seemed, when I questioned myself, Myself would always think up answers and give me explanations which I had never considered before. Strange as it may sound, these explanations and answers always made plenty of sense to me. The following dialogue of thoughts is what took place between Myself and I:

I: The Bible of today has only 66 books. The original books of the Bible numbered 366. What happened to the other 300 books?

Myself: The truth is, the devil extracted 300 books of this knowledge for fear that the people would wake up and see his dirty deeds and kill him in their hearts and minds.

I: Why are Negroes so ignorant of who they are?

Myself: You should stop and think and ask yourself more questions along this line. If you do, the answer would be very clear to you. But, to answer you truthfully and to your satisfaction, I think the first step to seeing the truth, as we said before, is to realize that you don't know anything. This attitude will humble you enough to learn something. The average Negro, such as the less fortunate ones that live in the ghettoes, suffers from the lack of education he receives. Throughout the years, he has not known any better. He has failed to realize that the planter was not always sure himself of what he was planting. I feel, in his sending you to prison, he planted the wrong seed in you. This is what I meant when I said, "We have all been a part of the devil's scheme at one time or another in life."

Then again, the Negro carries the mentally self-destructive seed which helps to make the physically self-destructive seed bear its fruit. This fruit is the fruit of ignorance. We know that one blind man cannot lead another blind man through an unfamiliar, booby-trapped maze, lest they both stumble and fall into destruction. I will never understand why the Negro goes through life listening to and following the advice of those who are as blind as he. The Negro never realizes the hazards of his spiritual blindness until he grows old or it is too late.

I: Please, tell me, ol' Soul of mine, just what is all this racial disturbance about, and why are the Negroes so dissatisfied today?

Myself: All this disturbance with the Negro today is the beginning of the fulfillment of the prophecy. I think much of the Negroes' dissatisfaction today is justified. I shall try to discuss these reasons with you, that you may have a better understanding and know the true facts.

    Like anything else in the world, everything has its good and bad features. This holds true for the Negroes and their easiness with being so discontented. Restlessness in the Negro has its advantages and disadvantages. The Negro man today should realize that it took longer than a day to build Rome. Black, brown, white or yellow, we should all remember that man is not infallible, nor is a man a God, nor can he perform the miracles of the Almighty, the Supreme Being. The Negro has no right to expect miracles to happen overnight.

    We all know that the Negro's conditions in this country are not as good as they could be. But, conditions are improving and are much better today than ever before in the history of this country. We know the white man has done us wrongly in years past—and in many cases is still doing us wrongly, today. If the Negro wants his intelligence to be respected by all, then he must realize that he cannot fight fire with fire. The wise man would try to put out the fire with water (the water of knowledge).

    Regardless of race, creed or color, we all want money, better living conditions, social esteem, and many other things in life which currently may be beyond our reach to possess. What right has the Negro to go about hating the world just because he was not born a scientist, a millionaire, or a college professor? The Negro should realize every person in the world may or may not be as great or as famous as they would like to be. Who knows, they may not be of the right class. Our forefathers knew: getting an education is the key to economic freedom. We have to return to those pursuits. For while being educated we, at least, will be provided the opportunity to compete, and the rest is on us. The beauty of this country is that everybody has the opportunity to become what they want. Just remember, the happiest people are those who think good, interesting thoughts. To develop interesting thoughts, time should be spent in good company, having good conversations or enjoying good books or good music. Then, Negroes would bring the effects of happiness to themselves and to others.

5. Transgression—of the Mind 93

I: I realize what you have said to be very true. I have asked myself many times, how can the Negro expect to achieve progress or peace of mind or know happiness in life when he feels sorry for yesterday, and, worries about tomorrow while, in reality, he is making himself miserable today—and each and every day?

        I don't believe anyone should have to tell the Negro that we reap what we sow in this world. Violence and destruction are of the devil and the motto of his twin, Satan. When the white man sees the Negro resorting to violent measures, he tells himself, those stupid ignoramuses don't know it, but they are only hurting themselves and killing any chance they might have to progress in this world. It will cost them more to live now than ever before. Their violence will be the cause of their future struggles. The white man does not care if the Negro destroys himself, because he knows that in the end, he will make the Negro pay for all damages, to boot—one way or another.

Myself: Yes, I am glad to see that you and I are in accord about these incidents. By the way—your ideas have brought yet another thought to me: The Negro in America should remember "A mule cannot pull his load while he is kicking, and he cannot kick while he is pulling his load." Likewise with the Negroes; why don't they stop kicking and start pulling their load over the mountains of adversity and into the meadows of progress? Instead of asking for jobs, why don't they create jobs for themselves and each other? Economic independence is one of the true keys to success and respect as a peoples.

I: Oh, yes, I agree, but you were about to tell me something else about the Negroes' discontent when the conversation drifted.

Myself: Well, it is really too bad that the good, righteous Negroes of this country have to suffer for the wrong and evil-doings of a few stupid and ignorant ones.

I: I admit that there are times when I observe the things some of my people do and I want to call them "Niggers" myself. We all know that the word "Nigger" means "a low or degraded person." Negroes who resort to violence and destruction through race riots and murder are putting themselves in the category similar to that of an ignorant, mental degenerate—not to mention, they are putting us all at risk. Negroes, who act like "Niggers," deserve to be called "Niggers" by all people, black or white.

After thinking all these things to myself, I became very tired and must have fallen off to sleep. The next morning I started to think over the discussion that Myself and I had. I was thinking to myself, if only there was a way for me to convey all this information to the American Negro and the general public, perhaps it might serve to bring about better relations amongst all people (not that we're trying to step on the toes of the U.N.) Although it took several decades to produce, I trust that's what we have presented below. What we have tried to do is to dissect the process of mind transgression occurring in each preceding story into its several parts. Bear in mind—not every story comprised each part, but a smattering, a combination of the parts is evident in each story.

Transgression Construct

This theoretical construct outlines the process of transgression within the mind from extrovert to introvert . The subtitles I've outlined served as mile-markers, which advanced me through each stage to the final point of enlightenment. In this construct, each step leads to the next, logically. For example, I achieved isolation through incarceration, both of which encouraged meditation. The incarceration, isolation and meditation led me to purification, because I was forced to admit the truth about myself to Myself, and so forth. Again, all that was needed was time, privacy, a desire to make the effort, my effort itself and Myself. Although mine began with incarceration, yours can begin in any space or facility which provides you with the required level of solitude—a solitude capable of inspiring pure isolation. Again, the following is a brief synopsis of the steps in the process:

1. **INCARCERATION** Brought about privacy and automatic isolation.
2. **ISOLATION** Brought about meditation. My isolation automatically encouraged my thinking process. It closed the door of the external world. It promoted solitude, whose emphases were: loneliness from separation; seclusion, during which time my mind activated self-revealing recollections; emergence—myself emerged as the conscious element of this experience.
3. **MEDITATION** It brought about internal cleansing and mental purification. It consisted of the following: profound concentration, penetration of mind over matter, spiritual awakening.
4. **PURIFICATION** It brought about the challenge: cleansing my mind of evil thoughts and filling it with good thoughts. It forced me to face myself and to admit the truth to myself about myself.

5. **CHALLENGE** It brought about my choice, the test of my acceptance or rejection of purification—for better or worse.
6. **CHOICE** It brought about my acceptance of truth and thereby, my perfection. It furthered my attempt to better understand myself.
7. **PERFECTION** My final objective: communication with the introspective world. Perfection is the ultimate, the ALL and ALL, THE SUPREME SOURCE OF POWER.

We entered prison as boys. We exited prison as men. What was it that transformed us? How did Malcolm X and I go into prison stubborn, hard-core hustlers and have one of us emerge a world leader, and the other emerge a totally changed man? What did we study? How did it happen? I cannot speak for Malcolm X; I can speak for myself only. The answer: both of us experienced a "transgression of the mind." In our prison lives we called it a "transgression." In his public life, Malcolm X called it a "transformation." I yet call it a "transgression," because I still see it as an involuntary passing over from conscious to subconscious mind.

"Transgression of the mind," a theory based on my personal experience, was a by-product of my incarceration. Of all I've endured, it was the one most painful experience, yet the one which made the greatest difference in my life. I've told you several stories. Experiencing those stories was like trying to get a "hand up" on a terrifying, multiple-armed, single-headed monstrosity—in absolute darkness the dark; however, within those stories lies the process of my transgression. Again, below I have outlined the several stages I was able to observe and notate which comprise this seven step process. What is listed below represents a further breakout of the earlier, abbreviated description of the steps. Again, if you thoroughly analyze the stories which precede both of these listings, you will discover these steps therein.

I. INCARCERATION

Professional people the world over rent or own places in the mountains to isolate themselves from civilization. Frequently, I've wondered what would lead people like Richard Evelyn Byrd (who died in Boston in 1957) to go on numerous expeditions to the South Pole. Often, their purpose boils down to achieving one or more of the following: to meditate, to concentrate, to fulfill their reason for being without external or mental distractions. Well, in my own right, I was a professional. Practicing my profession landed me in prison. And instead of experiencing the solitude of the mountains, I experienced the solitude of a prison cell. My incarceration, in and of itself, presented an isolation which encouraged one of two things: self-deprecation, or meditation. I chose to meditate. Self-directed meditating led to my purification from all my old, bad habits. My purification, in many ways, challenged me to raise all other areas of my life to this new level of being, and in each case I always had a choice to strive toward the mark of perfection.

II. Isolation

For me, the isolation of my prison cell closed the door of extroversion and opened the door of introversion. I had no other choice in isolation but to listen to what I heard in my head. What I heard was from within. Acknowledging what I heard within was most important. All I needed was time, privacy, desire, the effort, inner thought and myself. Isolation provided me the opportunity to make a connection between my subconscious and conscious mind. Around that time, I remember hearing the late Malcolm X's "take" on his incarceration. He said, "Many people are imprisoned within the walls of their own minds"—and yet might be living in paradise. At this time in my life, in part, he was referring to me: living within the walls of my own mind, incarceration and isolation went hand in hand. By the same token, one does not have to be incarcerated to have isolation. But one should achieve isolation from their surroundings in some way, shape or form to bring about concentrated meditation.

III. Meditation

For me, meditation through concentration resulted in placing me into a kind of trance. I would practice meditation daily—insensitive to my external surroundings. It was self-induced through laser-like, intensely focused mental concentration. I learned that trance, as an unconscious condition, has a connection to hypnosis and self-hypnosis. Using the power of suggestion to force myself into meditation also increased my susceptibility to hypnotism. (In fact I got so deep into meditation, I would try to listen for radio signals from outer space. I had heard someone was experimenting with it and thought I'd try on my own—with my own scientific instrument.)

I recall, during the first few months in prison, Charles O'Neil, Leroy Ferguson, the two Thaxton brothers, Malcolm X and I used to practice mental telepathy and clairvoyance at night. Of course, we didn't know what we were doing. At that time, we discovered some of the more extended uses of meditation and concentration. We experimented with sending mental messages to each other. The following day, we would discuss who sent whom what message and if it were received. Several times we were successful, hitting the nail right on the head. It scared us. This startling revelation forced us to give this process our deepest respect. Leroy, Charles and the Thaxton brothers, if they were alive today and read this book, would bear witness to this truth. Malcolm's famous quotation about the prison walls of your own mind was an important mental message. He was outright giving us a wake-up call.

My meditations were extremely important in the overall process of my mind transgression. I betrothed myself to my thoughts. My thoughts became more introspective. In order to meditate, I had to assume a mastery of self. Being incarcerated, the only place I could both seek and obtain any mastery was from within. (I am not referring here to forms of meditation which require chanting in a formal setting and prayer. The process I'm talking about could be spontaneous, almost instantaneous. To meditate, I simply had to concentrate and to engage my own thoughts. Profound thought, in and of itself a spiritual exercise and an education of sorts from within, focused my meditation so that I could perform the above-mentioned, telepathic exercises. But it was engaging in my own thoughts which led to deep introspection.)

In my meditation practice over a relatively short period of time, I was able to bring myself to a trance-like state rather quickly. This event marked a "graduation" in my meditation practice to abstract thought. For me, reaching this stage was like earning a symbolic diploma, representing the fact that I could now use my higher intellectual powers of mind. These mental experiences manifested themselves as truth from within. To think, what I discovered, was thought. Thought, I learned, is an idea and is theoretical or idealized. An idea is a mental image or conception. Thinking also is a form of metaphysical reality. Metaphysical reality, in the realms of thought, is ultimate reality. But ultimate reality is also a human perception. Thus, to meditate and to comprehend mental reflections as a practice, can help one achieve self-fulfillment, as meditation is fulfilling unto itself.

I also learned something about the partiality of ordered thought itself. I learned that thinking is an exercise where one uses one's power of judgment or reason over one's conception to reach a conclusion. For example, when one looks at a picture, one forms a mental impression which stems from one's imagination. Then one begins immediately to qualify both the picture itself and the mental impressions it evokes. These thoughts are colored, influenced or filtered by one's experiences (akin to the kinds of things Miles, Dizzy and "Bird" had done and were yet doing with both their "Bebop" and now their "cool jazz"—playing their soul, their spirit, as an extension of their thoughts). They are partial to who it is one has become in the world. They can even shape or predetermine who it is one will become in the world. (I hope we all see the need to keep our thoughts pure.)

Many, since our prison days, have said Malcolm X and I had experienced a transformation of our thought processes, that we had been rehabilitated. Through meditation, I insist, I experienced a transgression of the mind. For me, the words transgression and transformation have two distinct meanings. They are not to be confused with each other. Transformation means to convert conditions of personality and character; the complete undergoing of change of one thing to another. Transgression means going beyond imposed limitations of the law or commands of society, passing over the bounds of prudence (very much akin to passing over the bounds of conscious to subconscious mind). "Mind transgression" is a spiritual imbibing. It's like a quiet walk through your conscious and over into your subconscious mind. It's something I encourage everyone to try. It's a spiritually uplifting exercise, one that deserves an attempt by all who seek a deeper knowledge of self.

When I was in the streets hustling with Malcolm, I was living the life of the extrovert. I thought of my needs and desires foremost. In the world of meditation or introspection, I could go where I wished. Like the main theme in the poem "The Prison Cell" by Mahmud Darwish, my travels had no limitations. Malcolm X told the world of black people within the earshot of his voice, "You have been tricked, fooled and hoodwinked." And sure enough, we have. He very well knew what he was saying when he made that statement. It's a shame he and I had to go to prison to see all these things. Yet, life in prison removed our blindfolds. Having gained insight into these matters of life was to understand something we thought we had acquired in the streets but really hadn't. Yeah, we were hustling and doing quite well at it. But, if we were living on anything at all, we were successful due to both our individually and collectively strong survival instincts. I came to realize in prison I hadn't used my mind correctly when I was in the streets.

On the other hand, the perceptions I was coming up with in prison were true actions of my mind. To think back, to ponder the past, present and future are reflections of the world of the introvert. This is where I became aware.

Depending upon my schedule and circumstances on any particular day, I would fit in meditation—regardless of the time involved. I would meditate until I could feel, see and hear something from it. I paid strict attention, endeavoring to learn what was to be revealed to me. I could hear in my subconscience the old adage, "If at first you don't succeed, try, try again." From there, I would go to the next level of pure emptiness, and then into a dream state where time and space were both extended and one. I was learning to penetrate the barriers of the subconscious and to trust my instincts to the end. Keeping my mind's eye and ear open, my "inner self" became the professor. The first lesson I learned was how to communicate with my inner self. The hardest part for me was hearing through the silence. I was not used to silence in my life. To hear my inner self not only speak to myself through it, but also to correct myself was simply amazing. It was so easy—and free. Again, all I needed was a little concentrated effort, time, privacy and myself—nothing ventured, nothing gained. But the next step was the most crucial of all…

IV. Purification

In order to become purified, I had to make some serious changes. The greatest hurdle? I had to get my thoughts right. This was the step that was going to either make or break me in the process. I was about to cleanse my mind of all evil and immoral thoughts and egotistical ways of living, thinking, and being in my life. I had accustomed myself to practice severely undisciplined habits of mind. The first thing I had to do was to admit these personal violations to myself. (Complete honesty with myself was the key. To deceive myself, would have been to hurt myself, which I did not want to do.) If I couldn't face the truth about myself, to myself, then I had resolved in my heart and mind not to go any further. What I learned is that admitting these painful truths to myself presented me with a sense of freedom from guilt.

Once united with my thoughts, I began to see others and myself differently. I learned that the good I had seen and heard and felt from within overpowered any evil that dwelt within me if I followed it and stayed fixed on it. I saw that all the preparation I'd endured was necessary, for this was the most crucial step: purification.

I learned I could achieve purification only if I was sincere, only if from the depths of my heart I wanted freedom from the state of mind which landed me in prison. I'd come to learn that "thought," in and of itself, was freeing. Such was the type of freedom I desired—that which was not found under physical constraints or conditions. Younger than springtime, through this mental conditioning—almost like the more I worked it, the more powerful it got—my dormant spiritual nature had come alive. Becoming aware of its presence, I was then able to work with it, directing it outwardly, from the subconscious to the conscious mind. This power, this influence, manifested itself as a thought—*within the body*. It made me wonder if it were capable of being made manifest as a planet, a cosmos or a galaxy—*without the body* as a heavenly thought. What a powerful concept I had stumbled upon—all because I was brave enough to push myself to the extreme.

Extending these thoughts, I then pondered how some people travel the world over, seeking peace of mind and never finding or knowing mental serenity, when it's a quality of our spiritual natures which each of us carry within ourselves. "He that seeks…shall find." I found that what I had sought was within my grasp all along. I simply had to reach for it—within the deep recesses of my mind. There are no free lunches in this day and time. In order to purify my mind, I had to study my own emotional history. Through intense concentration, I had to bring all my mental eccentricities to the surface of my mind. Understanding the reason for their existence, I approached the realm of purification. I understood at this time why psychology is such a pure and fulfilling science. I found that in undergoing this process of purification, I was actually dealing with self-psychoanalysis—but on a spiritual plane, and all originating in my imagination. All those thoughts which I had repelled from my conscious mind at this time had come to the foreground, whizzing past my fixed lens like racing cars past the finish line on the track of my subconscious mind. These two entities, fighting constantly for preeminence in my body, is one reason I experienced the eccentricities and frustrations I did in my life—a cause and effect relationship of the physical and mental experiences I confronted daily. I learned that if I were not careful, this mental battle could result in a state of manic depression, or worse, psychosis or schizophrenia. Again, in order to unravel the mysteries hidden in my subconscious—which caused mystical mood swings in me—I had to go over my entire life, past and present. Then and only then could I see my future. This is where incarceration and isolation played their part in my life. I was very apprehensive about giving up my life as I knew it. Yet, I knew this task required (nay, demanded) sacrifice. That was my reality. Those were my fears. Fear in general is grounded in ignorance, and the fear of reality would have resulted in my nurturing an unfounded inferiority complex.

I realized I could not be too taken by the external world in order to practice my meditation. Regardless of how I did it, what was most important was that I did it by any means necessary.

Getting caught up in the external world in my life often lead to chaos and frustration and, ultimately, incarceration. Now, I'd found a way behind bars, to—as the R&B group Funkadelik would later say—"Free (my) mind."

As a result of these transgressions of my mind, I ended up finding myself behaving and thinking in "unorthodox" ways. These "abnormalities" provided a strong stimulus to the eye of my mind, my imagination, and it gave me a clear way of both perceiving and receiving the world, especially as it pertained to wisdom and knowledge—it caused me to feel like a complete stranger to myself. But all in all, through this process, I came to understand my own "aberrations."

My final words on this purification process are that ignorance as to who or what God is fed the fire of fear within me. I was a victim of distorted circumstances and choices in life, and didn't realize why. I felt like a caged intruder wallowing in the ruins of my pent-up emotions. Mentally and physically I had sought an outlet for them. Again, once I was incarcerated, I came to find my pent-up emotions were caused by both my discontented state in life and in my disillusionment with Christianity. My high-held ideals, although they were far beyond my intellectual reach, they were well within my spiritual reach. Reaching to them resulted in purification, which introduced the first two in a duo of final hurdles: challenge and final choice.

V. Challenge/Final Choice

To face my challenge, I realized I must have self-generated, intestinal fortitude enough to think positive under all circumstances, and to fight off all evil—mentally and otherwise. It was almost as if I were in a battle with truth itself—all the while being tested to the limit. Although I have always been intensely interested in mysterious, challenging phenomena, I had never before been put through such a tough, intellectual gauntlet like this. Of course, I realized I was being challenged to take my life to a higher level, and this challenge required that I immediately start making choices, right and wrong.

At this point, a verse from the Bible came to me, "Man cannot serve two masters. For he will love one and hate the other." I discovered the same thing when I realized I had to accept or reject either the truth or the lie of my life: and accepting, I found Heaven, introducing peace and paradise to my life. If I had rejected the truth, there is no question in my mind, I would have gone straight to Hell (literally, metaphorically and physically) until I perished, utterly. The Heaven I speak of here is tranquillity and the ability to transgress within our minds, at will. I found that to live, hear, see and feel all that is meant to be known in the world of truth, came from within me. In order to facilitate this process internally and externally, I had to have my mind and body free from any and all frustrations. Frustrations were like a spiritual distraction. Ultimately, the decision of challenge, choice and change in this life is each of ours alone to make—regardless of the crosses we have to bear.

In the final stages of this level, I faced challenges from those around me who were resigned to cynicism and defeat. I found they feared my gain in life would be their loss. Often I discerned jealousy in their actions towards me and others. Yet, in the face of these challenges, I had to remain steadfast, consistent with the choices I had made.

Living and learning from—and how to perform—"mind transgression" was like engaging in an aerobic exercise. The more I forced my body to endure, the more "in shape" I eventually became—both from the outside in, and the inside out, and my "shape," as ever-expanding as the universe, had no conditional limits. In undertaking this process, I found it most important to hear, to see, to understand and to obey the commands I received. Perfection exacted a price. Right choice and final action were but a few of its demands.

VI. Relative Perfection

In speaking of perfection as a superior quality of life, I will use as a point of reference perfection as it relates to me as an individual.

Perfection in this case ultimately will refer to my recognition and acceptance of truth. Although truth is relative, and one man's truth might be another's hypocrisy, I'm speaking here of those universal truths which speak to the soul: truths as obvious as light and darkness, perfection and imperfection, sin and holiness, etc.

I saw perfection as a Polaroid print of truth, an indisputable fact. I had come to see, for the first time, what was meant by, "God made man in His perfect image." But my vision went beyond that. I saw perfection as an agreed upon standard of character and as a way of being in the world. I saw perfection in the world into which I was planning to re-emerge some four years later as an act of faith; faith, because my perception of the reality of perfection in nature—both geophysical and social—required a trust, and its continuum, a confidence that I couldn't prove or demonstrate by any logic I could conceive. Through transgression, I found it was possible to attain social, religious and moral perfection. Being the very best one can be in every way represents the highest degree of proficiency and excellence one can achieve on an individual basis. (In fact, in society, some people are referred to as, "Your Excellency," etc.; aside from conferring upon them respect, this term also means: "extraordinary, superior merit, eminence" and "remarkably good.")

I am a man born free, of lawful age and proud to be black. I consider myself to be the equal of any mortal man, be he a king, president or potentate. Yet, I recognize that in attaining a level of spiritual excellence, forgiveness—of both others and self—has to be a part of the equation.

Still, I wrestle with people like the judge and district attorney in my 1945 case. (They exercised racial prejudice, bigotry and inflicted upon Malcolm X and me misery and pain unfairly. They are no better than the liars and con artists who want to bilk the unsuspecting masses of their possessions. They are no better than unscrupulous professionals who want to peddle "bills of goods"—from "electric shock treatment" and placebos, to land in Florida.) I still find it hard to respect or to address people like that by such lofty titles as, "Your Honor, Your Excellency, Your Eminence, " etc., because they, in certain instances, apparently refuse to carry the mantle with the authority, fairness and "excellence" with which they've been entrusted by the people.

At times, while engaging in these mental exercises, I felt like an alien. Remember, we were doing all this in 1945–46. Today, New Age spiritualism has sprouted all manner of alternative religions, fads, cults, you name it. But indulging in this deep, meditative practice in the middle of a hard-core state prison, which, by the way, housed an electric chair (in the "Cherry Hill" section of the prison) in 1943, was no laughing matter. Sometimes, I felt I was from Venus, and the non-practicing inmates from the Amazon. Although we were in the same place, we were not "in the same place." Or still, a better example: if two different types of guys (one dysfunctionally aggressive and the other equally passive) were to go to an art film, you could bet they would not see the same movie—even though they might have been sitting in the same row and have been at the same show at the same theater. Frankly, despite my tremendous "transgression" discovery, I was afraid to apply these principles in my life around people who were ignorant of what I'd discovered to be my "personal truth" in living. I realized then, that my life would have to be my testimony of perfection and truth. The results would have to serve as self-explanatory principals, and speak in both a provocative and a powerful way. They would have to "show," not "tell."

In this transgression of my mind, I conversed with my higher, inner self. In such a communion, I received the answer to all manner of questions. For example, that's when I discovered perfection's role in the cycle of life as being our advancing from nothing, becoming something and returning to nothing: 360 degrees of "ashes to ashes, dust to dust," nothing more.

The process I undertook whereby these truths were revealed to me was almost like engaging in the process of osmosis where learning, knowledge and physical evidence of mental phenomena is made manifest during sleep. For example, just before going off to sleep, in a conscious/semiconscious state, I would make some demand of either myself, life itself, anything. Within weeks, I would see results. It was that simple. It's almost as if I was actually reclaiming my higher self both from myself and from society, and launching it into a pure spiritual realm, in search of a truth which it would be charged to make manifest in my life. Having said that, I must admit, ultimately, "transgression" is just one of those processes which defy real scientific explanation because it is a process which does not exist in the scientific realm.

Humbly, in the above pages I have just attempted coaching you in the process of "mind transgression." I am unable to explain the process with any more clarity and detail than that which I have provided.

Yet, I submit, experiencing a transgression of the mind is an honorable achievement. The experience is worthy of a proclamation, or a public ceremony. Having acquired this level of understanding, or this state of being in the world, through positive thinking and a code of ethics, is not only exciting but also worthy of recognition of some sort.

My faith and belief had earned me spiritual fulfillment. (Mine was like a "Pilgrim's Progress," of sorts.) From birth, I learned as an infant to communicate instinctively by means of repeating sounds I heard from my parents. Through these repetitions, I learned the use of language. As I grew older, I gained mastery of the discipline of language through a conscious effort, which included developing speech, sound by sound and word by word. As an adult, in developing this transgression of the mind process, I felt like a child, even though I (again, at this point as an adult) had the capacity for thought and communication on a more abstract and sophisticated level. Striving towards, and achieving mastery of mind transgression, I thereby emerged to become a prime example of what all human beings, rising above the level of our animal existence, can achieve. I had in my possession one of the symbolic keys to success in life: through knowing myself, I had transcended myself. You can, too.

I trust I have shared this key with you in such a way that you can use it. If you do, use the key wisely.

6

The Black Man and Christianity

Telepathically, the world has been put under a spell called, "Religion." As a result, the world will not progress until it comes out from under that spell.
Religion is a money-making institution, nothing more.
For "Religion's" prejudice toward minority races world wide, has proven, through its current practices, it is not a divinely inspired path upon which to tread.
Religion is not supposed to honor racial prejudice. Christianity, for example, teaches us to love our brother. Anything which teaches otherwise is not "of Christ."
Yet, the contemporary practice of Christianity where segregation rules (as Malcolm X said, "America's most segregated hour of every week begins at 11:00 A.M., every Sunday morning!"), makes of Christianity a contradiction to all mankind.

—*Malcolm "Shorty" Jarvis*

THE SERMON

I'd rather see a sermon than hear one any day.
I'd rather that you walk with me, than merely show the way.
The eyes are a better pupil, and more willing than the ear.
Good council is confusing, but examples are always clear.
The best of all the preachers are the ones who live their creed.
To see their good in action is what everybody needs.
I would learn how to do it, if you let me see it done,
For seeing your hands in action is better

than following your tongue.
The lectures you deliver may be wise and true,
But, I'd rather learn my lessons by observing what you do.
I may understand you, and the high advice you give,
Yet, there's no misunderstanding, how you act and how you live.
—*Adapted from the original by Malcolm "Shorty" Jarvis*

The Nation of Islam has my deepest respect, because they are the only people I see today putting forth a supreme effort to raise the social, economic and spiritual consciousness of black people from the grave of ignorance and stupidity—physically, mentally and morally—to "a live perpendicular on the square of life, wisdom and knowledge."

Theological studies have proven every race of people have their own form of religious beliefs. As a generalized majority, the Chinese believe in Buddhism; Jewish people believe in Judaism; Africans, Ethiopians and Arabs believe in some form of Islam. Most white races of people believe in some form of Christianity. Likewise, the average black man in America has believed in Christianity from the days of slavery right to the present time. My own family believed in it. Common sense should tell any black person that their religion should be that of the majority of the world's black people, Islam, or some form of African religion. I have said, "Christianity is incapable of ensuring equality, dignity and justice to the black people of the world," both because it's not our inherent religion and because of the ways it's practiced.

We lost our identity as a people in the "Middle Passage." We have become a race of invisible men. We have to travel back through our "Middle Passage," tunnels of ignorance to retrieve our identity; for what we have lost is our birthright, our natural inheritance.

For example, while it is morally bound to be forthright, to the black man, Christianity has been evasive. Historically, its believers have been separated and divided along the lines of skin color—among other similar superficialities—for years. Its declared mission is supposed to be brotherhood, via the Christian faith, and in the name of Jesus Christ. Unfortunately, it appears "love," in Christianity, is not a God-given birthright for black people, to be shared with the black race. Love, in Christianity, is for white people, for the white race—if you don't believe me, go visit a suburban church on a Sunday morning.

In addition, Christianity incorporates many fraternal brotherhoods in which the black man is neither wanted nor welcome. This fact alone should open a blind man's eyes. What is wrong with the black man? He walks about like Hiram of Abiff, wandering around like a zombie in a winter's wonderland, never seeing, never learning, never hearing the truth, completely dumbfounded, stumbling along as blind as a bat in the daylight. When will the black man realize the blind cannot lead the blind, lest both fall into the pits of Hell?

On page 347 of Alex Haley's *Autobiography of Malcolm X*, Malcolm was right on target when he said, "America's black leaders' most critical problem is a lack of imagination. Their thinking strategies are limited basically to those ideas or issues which are advised or approved by the white power structure." The American white power structure doesn't want the black man to start thinking. If he does, and it shows in his deeds and actions, he is considered dangerous and a threat to them. Should he grow big enough to think internationally, that becomes his death warrant, and he must be eliminated as was Gandhi, Malcolm X, Martin Luther King, and so on. Prior to Andrew Young—who couldn't last—no other black person in the USA has been ordained by our government (has received carte blanc, diplomatic approval from the State Department) to indulge in federally-sanctioned and endorsed international affairs of State, worldwide.

I mentioned back in Chapter Two, how my grandfather helped lay the cornerstone of the Union Baptist Church in Cambridge, Massachusetts. I am the first in my family to deviate from the family tradition of practicing Christian beliefs. (Once again, all this because of what the judge and district attorney said and did to Malcolm and me during our trial.)

We all know the Ku Klux Klan's symbol is the burning cross. How does the white man expect the black man to believe in the cross as a religious symbol when he burns it? By so doing, he has shown the world, by his own admission, that he does not believe in it. He has told the truth about himself through his actions. But still, it appears black folk need a hearing aid to get the message.

The cross is a symbol with many meanings, chiefly that of death. Turn it sideways, it means possible death at a railroad crossing—if you don't exercise caution. Over church buildings and so-called Christian temples, it still represents death in a physical and mental sense. When framed by "religion," the teachings received in these buildings are misleading, confusing, and, in some cases, are the cause of psychological frustration, and mental death.

The white power structure, through its use of Christianity, has the black man on his hands and knees, looking to the sky for his utopia, paradise, and that which will not exist for him in this world via Christianity, as practiced by the "power brokers." Black people are being robbed of their human rights. The "powers that be," through their system of taxes, welfare and unemployment have their hands in our pockets, and their foot you know where. In the USA there are still states which covertly uphold discrimination, segregated laws and white supremacy—not all of these states are down South, either. For example, well into the 1950s and early 1960s, blacks in Washington, D.C., this nation's capitol, were summarily not served at kitchen counters in certain areas (like the Wisconsin Avenue, Georgetown and Connecticut Avenue areas—to name just a few). We need to wake up and smell the coffee! (The Jews of the Nuremberg Trials knew how to do it. They knew what time it was. But black folk have swallowed the bait—hook, line and sinker.)

In western civilizations, it is customary to wear black for family death and mourning; the supposition being black represents death, mentally and physically. I find it interesting that in far eastern civilizations, the reverse is true. White is the color representing death and mourning, not black.

The "Establishment" has taken the black man's stupidity for granted. Abraham Lincoln said, "You can fool some of the people, some of the time, but not all of the people, all of the time." For example, how many of us have thought through the dangers of alcohol? Our prevalent consumption pattern should serve as a red flag signaling our lack of control over this deadly disease. In some communities, the scope of this problem bears a multigenerational scar: a liquor store on every corner; homeless alcoholics, everywhere; blighted communities; an apathetic citizenry—alcohol is our cross to bear, our Mt. Everest to climb.

Alcohol is called "The Devil's Brew." Knowing what it is, why do so many black men (and, surprisingly often, Christian men) drink it? It dulls both the brain and one's thinking ability. Who makes it and why? THINK. Is it an element of the devil's control? What we believe and have faith in is largely responsible for both what we do and the effects of those actions.

We ponder and wonder, what is wrong with the younger generation of today? The black man's belief in forces outside of himself (like those icons prevalent in Christianity) has set him backwards in life, and it's the cause of his mental, physical and moral degradation. One of the Ten Commandments is: "Thou shall not bow down before a graven image." The cross, being a symbol of death, with the body of Jesus Christ impaled to it, makes of it a graven image. To worship a graven image is idolatry, and idolatry is akin to devil worship. The black man's big problem is, he's afraid to be himself, that is, mentally and physically black. The "Uncle Toms" and handkerchief-head, coffee-drinking "Hirams of Abiff" go along with the white man's caste system, thus making white their graven image, their Holy Grail. The role portrayed by Uncle Tom is representative of an attitude amongst blacks which persists even to this day.

I know now what Malcolm X meant when he said, "You have been tricked, fooled and hoodwinked." Martin Luther King, Jr. preached, "We shall overcome." He knew what he was saying, but he didn't finish the statement. He should have said, "We shall overcome ourselves." The white man's claim to fame is white for white. The black man's claim should be black for black. In many cases it is not. Too often, blacks make that claim for whites. The black man needs to smarten up, transgress, clean up his act, and walk upright among the enlightened. Black people's ancestry traces back to Africa. Africans are well-versed in human and spiritual sciences. Psychology had its origin with the Egyptians and Africans. It was referred to as "Study of the Soul." But, pain and torture came to my people when they were taken from their natural cycle of "360 degrees of life," and denied their sacred rights as human beings. Even more, we were looked upon by our oppressors as animals. Considered as inferior as a low-life beast we were bought and sold into slavery. The lineage of African kings and queens was paraded, like the naked and the dead in spirit, at humiliating auction blocks, and bargained for by our oppressors like cattle. That's the real heart of the matter. Furthermore, after receiving our emancipation, we expect this oppressor, who once owned us like a donkey, to now treat us like all of his sons? The black man better wake up.

In fact, I remember once while I was in prison, pondering this question for the first time I heard that Malcolm X had been transferred to the prison colony where I was. I thought, once I explained to him what I was searching to find out, he might help me to sort things out in my own mind. After all, two heads are better than one. A few days later, Malcolm and I had our heads together, and to my surprise, he told me plenty about what I wanted to know. I will never forget what he presented to me.

"Everything in this world comes in pairs," he said. He then went on to discuss morality, immorality, truth and lies, God and the devil. He then asked me, "Are you good or bad?"

Naturally I said, "I try to be good at all times."

He said, "Good! Know that the black people symbolize good and the white people symbolize evil."

At first I was shocked to hear this and didn't believe it—despite my feelings about the judge and the district attorney. I was still confused, and must have appeared so. Malcolm, detecting my confusion from my facial expressions, continued.

"Tell me," he asked, "when you look up in the sky, what do you see?"

"Nothing but space," I answered.

He asked, "What color is the sky?"

I answered, "Blue, of course."

Malcolm then asked, "Then you admit that there is nothing but a vastness of space and eternity up there, and space makes the sky appear the color of blue?"

"That's right," I answered.

"Then tell me," asked Malcolm, "How can anything live or exist in space, even God?"

"That," I answered, "I don't know. But I would like to find out."

"I will try to explain," said Malcolm. "You just said that space was nothing, and you don't realize it. Everything you were ever taught about God being in Heaven and the devil in Hell was symbolic."

"Symbolic of what?" I asked.

"Of everything right here on earth," said Malcolm. Then he went on to explain. "According to the *Winston Dictionary*, it says that the word 'blanc' or 'blank' means colorless, pale, and white. The French word for blanc or blank means white."

"According to the dictionary" again, I say, "Nothing, is that which is nonexistent, a person of no importance, or significance; that which is without quality or magnitude; that which is void; a vacancy or emptiness. Apply these descriptions in terms of people, and there you will have your answer as to what a white man is. The only people in the world who are pale and colorless are the white race of people. You just said yourself, that anything 'blanc' was nothing. What does this make the white race of people?"

Malcolm answered: "If and when you see a white person with brown eyes, you well can believe they have some of the black race of people's blood in them. If not, they may be a black person with real light skin passing for a white. You and I know there is no living form of human life in the ground or in the sky. Therefore, Good and Evil must be elsewhere on the face of the earth. The Holy Scriptures tell us that the devil lives on the lust of the earth and his evil doings. Never before in the history of the world have there been so many wars and evil forces alive and at work. The people who rule the world at present are directly responsible for these evil forces of destruction. In the past it has been well within the white man's power to maintain peace in the world. Why hasn't he done so? This fact alone should prove, too, that the white man is evil. Only the devil himself could think of evils of destruction like the atom bomb and many other nuclear horrors, which have all the world in constant fear of total destruction. To simplify all that I have said, God and the devil are right here on the face of the earth."

Then I asked, "Where is God?"

He explained, "God is you and every black person. You see? The word 'God' does not mean a superhuman being that lives in the sky as a vast majority of people, through religious teachings and popular conception, are led to believe. The word 'God' is more or less a title. For example, thousands of years ago, and in some countries today, people are called lords and gods like we apply the title to certain people in professions like doctors and lawyers. But, God in the sense I am referring to it, is your soul, your feelings, your subconscious mind and your understanding. For this reason you have heard people say all your life, 'God dwells within you.' This is what your soul meant when it said to you, 'The key to all success lies within your own soul.' The only people upon the face of the earth to possess these divine qualities of God are his chosen people, the black people. According to the *Winston Dictionary*, God means: One Supreme and Absolute Being, the Creator and Preserver of the Universe. Now we all know that the atom bomb and other nuclear devices are capable not only of destroying our world, but the universe also. I ask you, how would you personify the man or race of people who hold this power in their hands—as God or the Devil? This is really something to think about. Are they good or evil?

"Theologically, God means the Creator, Ruler. All-powerful and all-knowing and all-good. Use your common sense and reason for yourself. Is there the slightest possibility that the things that represent God could be attributed to the white man? Incidentally, God and good mean the same thing. In the *Winston Dictionary*, the word good means that which gives pleasure, that which is full or complete, reliable, honest, genuine, virtue, that has excellent moral qualities: pure, kind, merciful, gracious; that which is desirable; excellent; righteous; just; and honorable. How can any man in his right mind ever say any one of these vivid descriptions can portray the white man, who's all but annihilated our race?

"I certainly can't," I said.

"Why?" asked Malcolm.

"Well, the way the white man has ruled the world is the real reason, in my opinion," I said.

"This is why there is so much racial hatred and vicious wars which destroy innocent lives," said Malcolm.

"I can understand now," I said, "why some white people mistreat and even kill black people every chance they get. Your information explains the motives of white people's discrimination and exploitation of the black people."

"It explains why white people oppress black people socially, politically, religiously and economically. The facts should also explain his motives for using white supremacy to undergird his ruling of the world. The white man knows all these things concerning himself," Malcolm said.

"From now on, just remember that all popular conception is false, and also remember that everything in this world exists in terms of black or white, right or wrong, good or evil, and you will be the wiser for sure. It's an impossibility for a person to walk two ways at the same time. So black is black and white is white, and never can the two mix."

What a powerful conversation. Malcolm would then later go on to both develop and then to share some of these ideas with the world. These thoughts and others of his thoughts and actions are directly responsible for his premature death.

Suffice to say, today, for our own edification, we should feel obliged to develop our minds. We cannot and should not expect the same people who stole our minds, our languages, our culture, to return them to us. That is not going to happen, nor can we expect to either be given or to be taught the truth about our history. If you want it, you must seek it to find it. Meditation, study and research is what is needed to elevate ourselves. We are informed about where the wisdom and knowledge is when we are told to travel East to find it. In Africa resides the source of wisdom and knowledge. Let it be your guiding light.

Leaders in the northern hemisphere have used both their war machines and Christianity to lay claim to their position of world leadership and domination of southern hemisphere countries—despite the fact that southern hemisphere populations double and triple their own, in size. Geographically speaking, it is time we minority races claim our birthright. It is time for a change. For the benefit of all people, that change must take place right now, not later. Later may be too late. We must advocate peace or we will all "rest in peace."

The ruling class, on a worldwide level, needs a "changing of the guard." The bureaucratic bigots, worldwide, who make and control the laws we have to live by, have to go. We need what they used to call a "guard of honor." We need black folk who know what time it is, not like some of the shams we experience today—certain black folk on the police force acting far worse than any white man ever thought to act. We don't need any more black folk being used as a "front" to continue the misrepresentation of truth, justice and the African Way. Let it be clear, what I advocate is not hatred for the white race of people. I am simply telling the truth about the situations and conditions that do exist. I advocate, simply, love of the black man, for the black man.

In the year, 1947, while my mind was still floating in deep, cosmic concentration and meditation, I wrote the following article. I called it, "Ending of the Christian Era."

> Astronomically, and in stellar history, the Christian era will end fifty years into the 21st Century. Signs of the gravest danger multiply in the world—especially within western civilization. Ideals, principles, and faith in humanity are disappearing... Jim Crow ...Communism... Apartheid ...and Ethnic Cleansing...(all pointing to the same thing: segregation) have been the "order of our day." People have no respect for each other. We have embarked upon an age of nihilistic decadence. Unless the torches of true freedom and humanity/brotherhood can be re-ignited, the true spirit of freedom, justice, and equality for all within the construct of western civilization will pass with the Christian era. Astrologically, historically and astronomically, that period ends with the sun's passing from the Zodiacal sign, "The Fish," into the sign, "Aquarius," or the water bearer. Water, symbolizes wisdom and knowledge. We had better drink of it—before it's too late.
>
> Christ was born about 2000 years ago, give or take a few years. His birth ushered in the beginning of the Christian Era. At that time, the sun entered the zodiacal sign of the "Fish." (It takes 2000 years for the sun to pass from one of the 12 zodiacal signs to the next zodiacal sign.)

The fish, which ushered in the nascence of Christianity, is still one of the many signs in the zodiac. The symbol of the fish is found in and on the tombs of many of the early Christians, on lamps and other objects—especially in the catacombs of Rome. (These catacombs housed the first great underground cities. They provided protection from war brought by enemies. Later, they served as the forerunners of air shelters for many centuries.)

Astrologers, philosophers, astronomers and historians hold that the transition of the sun from one zodiacal sign to another, at 2000 year intervals, is always attended by great events such as the birth of Christ; great spiritual or intellectual movements—whether they be up or down the scale of progress; by reforms and new ideas; by historical, political and revolutionary changes in the world. These changes begin 50 to 100 years before the sun's final transition into another zodiacal sign. The institution of Apartheid in South Africa legalizing segregation while making inter-racial marriages illegal, Bull Connor and the Civil Rights Movement...The rise of Soviet Russia and Communism to a world power, the conquest of 500,000,000 people in China by Communism, America's taking over of world leadership, the great struggle between the East and the West, the rising danger of Communism to western civilization (as well as its demise), and the coming transition of the sun from the sign of the "Fish," to "Aquarius"—and with it a number of changes—the growing economic distantiation between Northern Hemisphere and Third World, Southern Hemisphere countries, all are signs of the coming of the New Millennium.

It's been said, "Each generation shall become weaker but wiser." Through their use of education and modern technology, the younger generation has become not only very wise but also very weak. They have acquired knowledge, but many of them do not put it to good use. "Generation X's" trademark has not been either their spirituality or their use of wisdom, but rather, their yielding to all manner of evils and temptations—and all from the external world. And if the children are our future, then for the second time in two thousand years, Christianity and all that it implies is in the gravest peril.

The first peril was Mohammed and the fiery, fanatical spirit of militant Islam. That peril lasted over seven hundred years, from the 7th to nearly the 15th Century. The Christian Crusaders failed to gain the Holy Land—as Palestine was called in those days. They also failed in their purpose: to regain the Holy Land for Christianity. (Even when the British mandate over Palestine ended, the Jewish State of Israel was proclaimed. It's almost as if it just wasn't meant to be.) Muslims spread Islam 2000 miles over North Africa, conquered Spain and maintained its practice there for 700 years.

In central Europe, the Germans, Austrians, Poles and Lithuanians held back this eastern flood of Islam throughout the centuries. Those barriers have been swept away since that time. They were destroyed by the spread of democracy by "Superpower," Christian nations—who now find themselves in the greatest danger as a consequence of their blindness and secrecy. Through their consensual and silent church and state alliances and their collectively conscious, international benign neglect, most of these western nations were indirectly in cahoots in the creation of the most destructive thing on Earth, that death-dealing bomb. At the time, being touted in defense of the "Christmas Tree Institutions," the bomb was, and still is, utterly in conflict with all Christian principles and ideals.

In August of 1945, the late President Harry Truman gave thanks to God for the Hiroshima bombing which killed 180,000 to 200,000 people—and wounding more. The nuclear bomb, with all its overkill capacity about which scientists and congressmen spoke at the time, was and still is the most eloquent symbol of the peril in which America and the world find themselves, today.

Western civilization's Christian Era and its great achievements representing intellectual and materialistic progress are in peril from both external and internal forces. The nuclear bomb, chemical and biological agents of war and other such destructive devices America has developed, are but a few of these great antagonists. But our own fear and paranoia about each other is the greatest of these antagonists. This kind of paranoia sprouts things like: Nazism, which incubated The Holocaust…Ethnic Cleansing campaigns and the like…

Never before have there been so many religious denominations, churches, sects and cults squirming in an "inspired" labyrinth along divine "paths to Heaven…" Never so much talk of man's humanity and inhumanity to mankind…Never so much talk of laws, yet so much crime…Never so many organizations and secret societies to establish world peace—with words only…Never before so much preparation for war on a massive scale by so many countries…Never, never before has human life held such little value…Never so much education, so many schools, colleges, universities and so little true knowledge or wisdom (for a pervasive mediocrity engulfs the world's institutions of government, media and education, as original thinkers anywhere are few and far between)…Never in history such boundless generosity and magnificent programs like Ralph Bunche's Arab-Israeli Armistice or America's millions given in foreign aid in the Marshall Plan, or individual, philanthropic acts (such as that most recently demonstrated by Bill Gates—college scholarships for students in need)…Never such forgiveness of our debtors as the billions owed to the USA after three wars…I'm amazed that Americans still are giving freely of themselves today, to aid their brothers in programs like the United Way, the Red Cross and Habitat for Humanity, while on a more personal, utilitarian level, everyone wants shorter hours and more pay; no one wants to work anymore. If the individual is a direct microscopic reflection of the society, what do these statements say about what we are becoming?

And finally, our poor children. As we said earlier; they lack spiritual vision. They are, in effect, spiritually blind...They have knowledge but not true understanding. They know their future but not their past. They have no self love and they show little respect for the humanity of either their elders or their brothers and sisters. They should be the hope of our future. But if we were to get a glimpse of our future via the evening news, based on the way our children are presenting themselves, we would view our future with daunting hopefulness.

The solution is not force meeting force. That is a disastrous approach. Force redirected, is the key to survival. National strength, spiritually and morally, supported by both wisdom and knowledge is the key to world peace, national defense and security, and in this effort, our youth are our greatest resource. Having witnessed they are lost, we must teach our children to hold the torch if the torch will be passed into a new millennium.

To the Black man, all I can say is that, "the handwriting is on the wall." You had better wake up and discover your spiritual roots, and thereby discover too, the wellspring of your spiritual inspiration. Hammurabi, Hannibal, King Solomon, ours is a divinely inspired lineage. Previous comments notwithstanding—Alex Haley gave you the inspiration to find your clan in the Motherland. I hope that by the end of this chapter—or book—I will have given you the inspiration to discover their religion, to learn it, to learn its rituals and to practice it alongside the religion you now practice. Remember this: African religion is as adaptable as the air that you breathe.

Christianity is not the original religion of the Black man. His philosophy of life, his icons, and his religious practices are not steeped in the Judeo-Christian tradition. In fact, African religion is the original religion of man—if man truly originated in Africa and from the earliest of times practiced religion there. Literally, from the day of his nascence, man has worshipped God. That was one of his rituals of being, of living. As first man's experiences became more routine, worship ceremonies evolved to—in some way—acknowledge these events, these experiences in their history and in their cosmological view of the world. These rituals eventually found their way into first man's religion, expanding it and making it eminently relevant. (Due to the fact that they are grounded in the oral tradition, religions in Africa have never been committed to writing, as has the Bible. Nevertheless, judging from the historically-inherent inclination of the African to worship, it can be concluded that from the earliest of times he conducted some form of worship ceremony to his Highest God.)

Before Jesus, there were religious beliefs which were being practiced and upheld in Egypt, the Cradle of Civilization…The Nile Valley, the Fertile Crescent…a part of the African continent. After Judaism, all other religions not upholding the tenets of Judaism were considered "pagan, primitive." Was this viewpoint, a Euro-centric outlook, perpetrated since 1611 by King James and his appointed committee of English scribes for geo-political reasons while Britannia lay poised to—later in history— "Rule the Waves"? Is this opinion, this attitude, this outlook some sort of thematic carry-over from the Crusades? A well-veiled, cultural imperative, a divinely-inspired but a humanly-flawed manifesto justifying, through its placement in the Holy Scriptures, the spiritual supremacy of its practitioners? (In more recent history, the "Heliotropic Myth," a Euro-Atlantic cultural manifesto, steeped in self-serving superiority and based upon the idea that Euro-centric Western society was the highest and best that had ever existed, was supported by the tracking of human migrations and their relation to the movement of the sun from East to West. Yes, Britain lay poised to rule the waves for some time to come.)* In fact, some, in approaching the Bible objectively, approach it as literature first, history secondarily and finally as a book of wisdom and knowledge, and not as an indisputable religious tome—like the masses do today. Their thinking is, that because of its history, its scriptural inconsistencies and implausibilities, one must not forget to, "tie up one's camel." I'm left to ponder, does this scenario reek of "set up" or, is there some validity to it? (Although it is inconsistent and in some areas questionable, nonetheless, the Bible contains some very meaningful truths, and it is one of the most significant documents in the history of Western man.)

I ask that question because when Malcolm X and I studied African religions, we found that most religions of Africa are quite similar to Judaism—and visa-versa. They differ from Judaism in that they are steeped in the oral tradition, and they practice "spiritual divining."

Since its inception, African religion was organically bound to the African way of life. Over the centuries, as a response to their circumstances and experiences (floods, famine, diseases, etc.) Africans, through

---

*Jan Willem Schulte Nordholt, The Myth of the West, Grand Rapids, MI: William B. Eerdmans, 1995, pp. 208–218.

these experiences, developed ritualistic reflections on and responses to both life and the universe, shaping and re-defining the boundaries of their religion. Again, by and large there are no scriptures or holy books in African religion. It is a religion practiced and expressed through praying, rituals, offerings, sacrifices, the observation of customs, festivals and so forth. It is the product of a rich cultural heritage including (and extending from thousands of years) the thoughts and experiences of their practitioners' forefathers, mothers, men, women and children who have gone on before them. Through these ancestors' beliefs, rituals and experiences, the modern day practitioner is enriched by a vast resource of collective wisdom and guidance. It is easy to see how endearing and how secure this religion can both feel and can be, in actuality. Their religion is still a part of the ritual of daily living in modern day Africa.

Their beliefs center on topics similar to any other religion. They include—but are not limited to: God, human life and its meaning, spirits, the hereafter, morality, social contracts, truth, justice, love, etc. Ceremonies are conducted by a spiritual leader responsible for the spiritual well-being of his constituents and whose job it is to carry forth the religious traditions of the village, tribe, etc. The closest to a collective African ritual African-Americans practice in this post-Christian era is that of the ritual of Kwanzaa.

Also, unlike western religion, most "primitive" religions include either a Shaman, or some other type of diviner or spiritual leader whose job it is to navigate the spiritual world. Often they are highly skilled—reared in their religious traditions through several generations. They are specialists, experts, the human "keepers of the flame" of their extensive religious heritage. In many instances, their comprehension of this realm enables them to know the future...to use spirits to do their bidding...to perform highly effective spiritual counseling for their people. Even today, African doctors heal with both medicine and herbs and other vegetation. It is said, that the best of these doctors are assisted by spirits which guide them in selecting the best medicinal herbs. This is an unknown world in purely Western medicine...Alas, it is a world shaped by the African cosmological view (in sum, a view where the physical world is seen through a spiritual filter).

Today, in Native American cultures, it is not unusual to hear of "Witch-doctors" settling disputes between families...or Voodoo priests (the Houngan) of Haiti (not to be confused with some of New Orleans' "Streetcorner Bone Men") performing mass healing rituals...For example;

for thousands of years, the Babalawos (Yoruba High Priests) of the Ifa Tradition (Ifa refers both to the God and to His oracle in this ancient African religion underlying Santeria, Candomble and Vodun) have provided readings to their constituents, which both predict and otherwise affect their clients' futures. In some cases, these results are achieved simply by creating a harmonious balance in the individual through sacrifice, ritual and prayer; changing their clients' behaviors today sometimes effects successful future outcomes in their clients' lives—often reflecting the self-same outcomes predicted by the Babalawos in their initial reading with their clients. The idea here is that by teaching their clients to accept the fact that if they work with, and not against, their body's energies they'll prosper; and if they ignore these energies, they'll suffer.

If civilization began in the Nile Valley in Africa, then the forebears of the African worshippers were the original man and woman. In this regard, concerning Ifa readings practiced since the dawn of time, some Africans have been "Transgressing" for years, if "Those who know," have believed in and have been yielding to or "crossing over" to tap into and be used as a conduit by a universal energy force. (That is the essence of the "Transgression" I attempted to describe earlier.) In fact, for centuries they have believed this energy force can be used arbitrarily by the practitioner for good or evil towards others.

Yet, to this very moment, all of this modern day healing (demonstrating the remarkably organic flexibility and adaptability of these "primitive" religions), these spiritually-based practices and observances of ritual are considered by most westerners—blacks and whites alike—as taboo. Why? What is so vastly different about the underpinnings of these African (and other "primitive") religions that makes them "lesser" or "low" religions? I can't find it.

Is it because African religion is extremely fragmented…because it has no paradigm? African religion is not a homogeneous entity serving all African nations. It developed as an extension of the culture of each practicing clan—along with all other aspects of their heritage—making it an entity of the particular clan within which it evolved. Therefore, it can't be proselytized due to its indigenous, organic, evolutionary nature. A person must be born into a particular group to follow the religion of that group. Even for Africans who migrate within the continent, it is very difficult to adjust to—or to adopt—the religious practices of a peoples of another religious group. In fact, when this happens, it occurs due to the fact that the migrated convert infuses their traditional religion with the new religion—similar to what occurred during slavery for many Africans.

Is it jealousy? In general, African peoples are inherently more religious than Europeans, more worship-centered. For example; in contemporary society, socio-economically deprived blacks in general praise God far more actively than just about all strata of whites—especially affluent whites. In addition, the very earliest of records of African history show that the Africans of Ancient Egypt were a very religious people—from the Third Millennium B.C. Mesopotamian (Sumerian) religious practitioners, and the New and Middle Kingdom followers of Amun, to the later, practicing Moslems.* To this day, Africans practicing their traditional beliefs are said to be very religious. Religion for Africans has been simply their way of looking at and experiencing the world—a world view, or, for lack of a better term, their cosmology. It permeates their life to such an extent that many African languages do not have a word for religion—although they do have words for religious objects, places, practices and ideas. It is no wonder that over 85% of the total African population practices either Christianity or Islam. (Of Africa's 703,090,000 million people, 341 million are Christians and 285 million people practice Islam, while only 70 million Africans are followers of traditional religions.) What's sad about these prospects is that Africans have forsaken their own true religion, in many cases, to adopt customs and rituals not germane to their own geo-centric cosmology (or, their localized world view) in many cases leaving a large gap between their spiritual and physical realities.

Further, some African peoples, like the Native American, have not severed their connection to nature, as most "First World" peoples have. They approach their local environment with reverence and awe not with a "Master of the Dew," controlling, destructive or exploitative mind-set. They see nature's species as equal to man with equal rights to co-exist; thus, from the "genesis" of their embrace with Christianity, African man has been out of step with his own indigenous cosmology. The outcome of their practice of Christianity has, in many cases, been that of destroying the underpinnings upon which their traditional beliefs are based. What's more, as seen through the lens of Christianity, their "Nature Mysticism" (as it is often called) appears as "primitive non-

---

*Brondon, S.G.F., gen. ed., Dictionary of Comparative Religion, New York: Charles Scribner's Sons, 1970, p. 74.

sense," and in a more extreme view, the "idolatry" of "depraved animists." To put it both simply and symbolically, it's like they have given up their African drums for Rock 'n Roll—and the band isn't even "playing their tune."

Upon closer inspection, I find African religions fairly complex systems of thought...Systems where beliefs, cosmology, myths, moral codes, and behavioral imperatives are all interwoven into a fabric which adorns and dictates both their religious ideas and their every action on a communal basis. (The community holds and practices the religious beliefs as a unit. There is no, nor has there ever been a "Billy Graham" or a "King James" of African religion; the practices of African religion are germane to both the current and historical needs of its local practitioners. The individual need not adhere to, or even accept all of their communal beliefs.)*

On a daily basis, the individual's practice of African religion is reduced to simplicity. Its practice is best typified by the lyrics of a contemporary gospel song as performed by the Richard Smallwood singers, "Everything That Happens, Praise Ye the Lord." Most Africans live in constant praise to their Creator—especially for those things which occur in their lives which they don't understand.

Further, the generic, hierarchical construct of a typical religion on the vast landscape of African religions might look like this—give or take one element here or there (Please, understand that in Africa, over 1,000 different languages are spoken—many of which are mutually unintelligible within the borders of any particular country. Also, numerous ethnic groups abound, each with their own culture and religion): at the head, there is a Creator (He responds to, and helps to "settle" man's existential anxieties, as man sees, but God reveals—although eventually the village priest would share this responsibility), joined by a Holy Ghost. These personages are attended by lesser gods who are followed by the ancestral spirits (Bear in mind, Africans do not worship their ancestors. They acknowledge their ancestors from 4-5 generations back, to the present. This acknowledgment could be something as small as demonstrating appreciation for their ancestors' former existence—something similar to what African Americans do during Black History Month. They may also build a shrine or leave an object on their grave—much like we all do on Memorial Day. But worship is out of the question), all of whom are followed by the evil spirits...(Historically

---

Smith, Jonathan Z. HarperCollins Dictionary of Religion *New York: HarperCollins, c. 1995, pp. 10-18.*

speaking, the world has never been viewed materialistically—in a purely western sense—in African culture, even though their spiritual world has always been closely tied to the material world. For it is in the material world where the spirits apply their powers. There exists here a symbiosis, as the minor spirits, extant in this world, who are directly related to the Highest God, must serve man as the Highest God's intercessor—both to exercise their powers and to gladden their hearts both through man's acknowledgment and through his support by his good works). Sounds like the fundamental construct of Judeo-Christianity to me (just substitute God, Jesus, the Saints and the Devil, respectively).

In fact, some have said that the reason why so many slaves took so easily to Christianity while in captivity in the New World was not because they'd lost their spirit and fell into submission, but because it was so close to their own traditional religious beliefs, it brought them spiritual comfort. How else could these strangers in a strange land create the music—the spirituals, in particular—the black preacher, the various denominational practices abounding in the black community from slavery to this day? They had the unique ability to adapt, ultimately, because their traditional pattern of trusting God and life allowed them to "transgress;" to adapt, to transpose or to move beyond their demands for freedom from their oppression alone, to another plane: to focus on seeking a higher purpose for their suffering—that of God's testing their mettle, His demonstrating His Love ("He chasteneth those He loves"—Rev. 3:19), His retribution, etc.

Lastly, African religion is no "low religion," nor are any other non-western religions which demonstrate rather sophisticated results in their practice. On the contrary, African religion is so broad and so resilient, it stretches to this day to adapt to and to embrace those events and circumstances shaping a new world. Every new circumstance, every communal experience and idea is added to enrich African religions—and in the case of Christianity even, each interested clan eventually absorbed this new "Christianity" into their well-structured systems of belief. Wisely, Alex Haley encouraged us to investigate our roots. In this New Millennium, I think it is time we discover more than the genealogy of our forebears. I think it is time we now discover the religion, or at least the spirituality of our roots—whatever that means for you.

Excerpt from *The Heritage of Nubia:* "Out of Africa: The Supurb Artwork of Ancient Nubia" by David Roberts pp. 90–101
Henry Mitchell, *Black Belief*, Harper & Row pp. 8–67
Jan Knappert, *The Aquarian Guide to African Mythology* pp. 1–19

7
"Pivotal Events"

Ambition is born in one's present and yet extends from one's past, for we all have a desire to be better than we once were. Ambition also stems from a desire for more of something we already have, for people living with goals to achieve in life live it with conviction.

One who walks truly in spirit will not fulfill the lust of the flesh. Yet, for "The Fallen," the path to be traveled to get out of Hell and mental degradation is open to all.

Look at what's wrong to see what is right. Look at what's right to see what is wrong. Life is a battle. To be prepared, one needs philosophical and intellectual munitions. If, " the mind is a terrible thing to waste," don't let your mind be the terrible thing, or, in this battle it will get wasted. Stay attuned to your higher thoughts…your higher power. External freedom from human restrictions is a perennial dream. But internally, there are no limitations or restrictions.

The salvation of the world is in integration or disintegration, not separation.

—*Malcolm "Shorty" Jarvis*

During the past few years, I have been invited to do many speaking engagements at schools and colleges. The number one question from nearly all the students who have asked questions at the end of these sessions has been, "Who was the first person to teach Malcolm X how to use his brain?" and "Who was the first person to tell Malcolm X about Islam?" I have always answered honestly and in all truthfulness, "It's not important who was the first, second, or from whom. The importance of it all is, both of us did listen that we might learn."

To the best of my recollection, the answer goes back over 50 years. What I remember is, it occurred in 1943, when I first met Abdul Hameed. It was he who introduced me to the Ahmadiyan (Ahmadiyyan) sect of Islam, from India. (This sect was established by Mirza Ghulam Ahmad in 1889, in the Punjab state of India. [*Dictionary of Comparative Religion*, pp. 49–50, 362–364]. He longed for a regeneration of Islam. He claimed to have received a revelation and, among other things, to have come as a messenger in the spirit of Muhammad. By and large his teachings, although orthodox, were well-received by intellectuals, but not the general Muslim populace. The sect currently claims a following of 10 million, worldwide. A core community of 4 million resides in Pakistan, which serves as the national headquarters of the movement [Mircea Eliade, ed. T*he Encyclopedia of Religion*, MacMillan, 1987, pp. 153–155].

As I said before, I tried to tell Malcolm about this version, but my encouragement fell on deaf ears, meeting with total rejection. To the best of my knowledge, no mention of any Ahmadiyan version of Islam was heard of in Boston until 1942–1943. The Nation of Islam's version, from the teachings of the Honorable Elijah Muhammad as acquired by Malcolm while in prison, was introduced to Boston by Malcolm X in 1952. Again, the Ahmadiyan version of Islam was known in Boston in 1942—ten years before Malcolm introduced Elijah Muhammad's version to the city—but was not accepted. To the best of my recollection, the first time either Malcolm or I heard mention of the names "The Honorable Elijah Muhammad" and "The Nation of Islam" was in the Charlestown prison, in 1946. They came first from his sister on a visit to the prison, and later from his brother, Reginald.

On page 328 of his autobiography, Malcolm made it clear that he knew and met Abdul Hameed before going to prison. His prison visits from Mr. Hameed were also mentioned. The Muslim prayer books— written in Arabic—Malcolm and I received were left at the prison for us by Adbul Hameed in 1947. Our first visit from Abdul Hameed came at the Norfolk Prison Colony in 1947. Abdul Hameed played a very important role in our lives while in prison. (I will never understand why Malcolm didn't say too much about Adbul Hameed in his book. Perhaps, being as involved in the movement as he was, Malcolm felt Mr. Hameed's version of Islam bordered on heresy. Only time will tell.) On his visits to us, Mr. Hameed would explain how to pronounce the Arabic words contained in those prayer books. We were also receiving, through the mail, words of wisdom, knowledge and encouragement from Mr. Elijah Muhammad in Chicago. In addition, we were still receiving information from his sister and brother, on a mouth to ear basis.

Malcolm's visits from his family were few and far between. The reason for these lapses was that most of his family lived out of state, making it difficult to visit. His sister, Mrs. Ella Collins, was his only regular visitor—when it was possible for her to do so. She was Malcolm's only Boston relative.

My family situation was completely different. My entire family was from Boston, making my visits from them more regular. In fact, I used to have my family visit Malcolm also, so these visits could be put on his case work record. I took this action to let the prison authorities know people outside were interested in both of us. Because of the interest shown to us from without, it helped us to gain respect from within the prison.

At this time, we continued to receive privileged information from both the Honorable Elijah Muhammad and Abdul Hameed. On his visits, upon entering the prison, Abdul Hameed registered as a Muslim Imam (Minister) of the Ahmadiyyan faith from India. He requested to see Malcolm and me at the same time. According to the rules and regulations of the institution, only a lawyer, clergyman or a minister could make a request to visit two inmates at the same time. Visits were otherwise conducted one-to-one. To our surprise, his request was granted on a religious basis. In the annals of the institution, this request was precedent-setting. It both set us apart and gave us instant credibility at the same time.

In addition, the laws of the prison stated, "An inmate must shave two or three times a week." Considering ourselves potential Muslims, we refused to shave on a regular basis for religious reasons. The deputy warden warned us, "abide by the rules and shave, or suffer the consequences" which were eight days on bread and water, in the "dungeon." We inmates called the dungeon "The Hole." Before being sentenced to The Hole, it was customary to have a hearing. At the hearing, the deputy warden was the judge and the jury on the matter. He was the one with the power of authority to sentence the accused to The Hole.

One day after having let our beards grow, we were called to the Deputy's office for a hearing. I was asked to go in first. Malcolm was told to wait outside the office. Upon entering the office, I was told to take a seat. I tried to relax myself, feeling I could think better by so doing; but instead, my mental guard went up. I thought to myself, this is a case where who you know outside would mean something. Taking my seat, a precautionary thought flashed through my mind, "It's not prudent to advertise to your adversary your capabilities, intentions or the extent of your intelligence. Let the element of surprise be your 'trump card.'" Another precautionary thought flashed: I felt it smart in this case to walk softly but to carry the big stick—of wisdom and knowledge—and to strike only to protect myself. Looking back over my months of confinement, I learned one thing in particular: to think at all times and under all circumstances. And I learned from Malcolm, "never let 'em see you sweat." I felt confident and prepared for anything the deputy was planning to throw at me. The following dialogue is what transpired:

Deputy: How are you today, Jarvis?

Jarvis: As well as can be expected under the circumstances one has to endure in prison, Sir. (Addressing him as "Sir," I thought showed respect for his position as deputy warden. Also, it demonstrated that I was learning humility—something all were looking for in me, especially after my courtroom performance.)

Deputy: In reviewing your case, it seems you are breaking the rules of the institution by not shaving. What do you say to that?

Jarvis: Well, Sir, I don't see where I am breaking any rules. There are approximately 1,500 inmates in this institution. About 900 attend Catholic services every Sunday morning. You provide a chapel for the Protestant believers to worship in, and you have made special accommodations for the Jews. They even have a rabbi attend their services. Every faith worships their God in their own manner. Many of us blacks are potential Muslims. Our faith is Islam. Our god is Allah. We are not provided with a facility to worship in. We believe in nature, and what grows by nature on our faces we will not cut or destroy. This is our way of paying tribute to Allah, our God. Do we Muslims have less of a right to pay homage to our god than do the Christians and the Jews? (That was the sixty-four-dollar question. Studying me with intense concentration, the deputy, absorbed in deep thought, became very quiet. I continued:) Because of rules and regulations are we to be religiously persecuted? (For the second time, within seconds, I hit him with another important question, and still no answer. I continued:) Sir, it's true, when we became prisoners we lost both our social rights and our physical freedom. However, convicts do have some constitutional and human rights. Freedom of religion is one of them—be it Jesus or Allah. You people do realize you put yourselves above God by forcing us Muslims to shave against our will? Should this be the case, I will have my family take this matter of religious persecution up with the Department of Corrections at the State House. Such an action could make things unpleasant for everyone, not to mention what would happen if the news media got a hold of it. They would have a field day with that news. We don't feel that we are breaking any rules or trying to make trouble for you people—or ourselves.

(I then mentioned the fact that Jesus Christ had a beard, and people believed in Him without condemning Him for His appearance. The deputy was stunned by this conversation he was having with a black inmate. He was taken by surprise and didn't quite know how to handle this situation. As the deputized head of the institution, he was in a precarious position. In all his years of penal work, he had never been approached in this manner by an inmate, black or white. He realized one thing and it showed on his face: he had to be very cautious in handling this situation. What with the press which had preceded our incarceration, he knew he was sitting on an explosive powder keg—this issue could have powerful international repercussions. The deputy finally answered:)

Deputy: I will look further into this matter. In the meantime, shaving will not be considered an infraction of the rules and regulations. You are excused, and tell Little he is excused also.

Malcolm, having overheard our conversation very casually said, "Jarvis, you're finally learning."

By the way—we never heard another word on the matter from the deputy. We didn't have to go to the Hole, and we didn't have to shave. Our beards grew.

It was just about this time (in 1947) that Abdul Hameed put in a strategic visit to the prison colony. His presence added more fuel to the above, volatile situation. His visit confirmed my remark to the deputy warden about possible religious repercussions—and maybe even on an international scale.

Without speaking a word, Abdul Hameed commanded attention wherever he went. He was like the "All-African Boy"—although not a boy by a longshot. He was a self-possessed man who walked tall with dignity and class. His general appearance was elegant. His clothes were immaculate; his shoes shined like a reflecting mirror. He wore a tall black fez which bore no insignia and had a long black tassel attached to it. Most people don't know what a black or a red fez represents or stands for. It represents 360 degrees of spiritual, physical wisdom and knowledge. People in positions of authority and people of the intelligentsia know this—especially men of the clergy, fraternal brotherhoods, politicians and those in the penal system.

Upon entering the visiting room, his appearance alone made us feel proud to have such a distinguished person ask for us. Sitting opposite each other, he instructed us to watch his back and he would watch ours. He told us to speak softly with our heads bowed over slightly to prevent security from trying to read our lips. The conversation was quiet, confidential and otherwise very secret. We could read in the faces of the prison personnel (and some of the inmates) that their curiosity was eating them up alive. For some reason, at this time, Muslims in prison were feared and not associated with. Black and white inmates segregated themselves from us, not us from them. The blacks that kept away from us did so because they had black skin, but (we felt) were white-oriented in their minds. They regarded Abdul as they would "The Iceman."

We had a code of ethics by which we lived in prison, and one of the things we wouldn't do was to solicit potential blacks to join us in "transgressing," or in practicing Islam. If they were interested in practicing the avocation of pursuing wisdom and knowledge, they were welcomed to join the flock.

At this time, the major concern—and worry—among the penologists of America was the growing rate with which black convicts were embracing the faith of Islam. (In time it would become customary that upon leaving prison fully qualified, an inmate would enter the Temple to become a registered Muslim. This policy came about several years after Malcolm's release, in 1952.) Since our prison term, the entire U.S. penal system has undergone a major change in its rules, regulations and policies. The legacy left behind by Malcolm and me set a precedence which to this day (many years later) has not been equaled.

Since Malcolm's release in 1952, most penal institutions have had their libraries well-scrutinized. Many books of wisdom and knowledge, ancient history, or simply important information have been removed. It appears this scrutinizing started at the Norfolk Prison Colony and spread all across the USA. The prison system is trying very hard not to spawn another Malcolm X, lest they live to regret it even more today.

Yet, life in prison, then as now, is not the worst thing that could happen to a person. For Malcolm and me, initially it would be considered a catastrophe, but eventually we would consider it a blessing in disguise. Physical imprisonment is one thing; however, mental imprisonment is quite another. It occurs within the individual. I would rather be in prison in body but free in mind, soul and spirit than to be free in body but imprisoned by immorality, bad habits of mind, and, because of my poor choices, miserable in spirit.

In Norfolk prison, Malcolm always used to speak of his lifetime ambition, which was to visit Mecca. When Malcolm made his pilgrimage to Mecca, he was confused—mentally disturbed and frustrated. Mrs. Ella Collins, his sister, was most probably the only person to realize how badly he needed that trip to Mecca. For this reason, she helped to finance his trip. On page 340 of his book, Malcolm said, "Never have I witnessed such sincere hospitality and overwhelming spirit of true brotherhood, as practiced by people of all colors and races in this ancient Holy Land of the Holy Scriptures. I am utterly speechless and spellbound by the graciousness displayed." He felt that he had been blessed to visit the Holy City, where he was treated like a king. And I am sure, that being the prince that he was, and surrounded by a blinding galaxy of "stars," that he'd added much by his own light.

He felt so good about the Hajj that he wrote a letter to the assistant head of his new organization, Muslim Mosque, Inc. His request was that the letter be made public so the U.S. news media could report his enlightenment. He wanted this to occur before his return to this country. He had his reasons, and I can understand why. I thought, long before this time in his life, his eyes had been opened to the reality of life. I admit, I was wrong. Of all people, I was amazed. I believe Malcolm said it all when he said, "I learned the truth in Mecca." The publication of his letter from Mecca did cause a lot of controversy. In fact, most people didn't believe he had experienced a change of heart—especially the white race of people. The mutual feeling among the general public was, the letter was a camouflage, a fake—indeed, a con or a hustle. He was still the same as he was before the trip.

I didn't take the same view on this matter as did the general public. I've never been one to line up in a queue with all the king's men and march to a beat. I've always heard a different drummer. I don't, like a blind horse, follow the conventions of those before me (society). Therefore, I would never subscribe blindly to the masses' train of thought on this matter. Malcolm's remark, "I learned the truth in Mecca," said more to me than what met the average eye and ear. I read it as an admission of guilt in the form of an explanation because, in his past life, he was incapable of seeing through deceitfulness. The Supreme Power knows I tried relentlessly to make him see a different point of view about people being people, regardless of race, creed or color. Once again, he flatly refused to hear this, saying, "Black is black and white is white, and the two will never mix." Looking at this comment from an experiential perspective, that remark is as bad as the one the district attorney made to us in court.

Needless to say, in many respects, Malcolm and I were exact opposites. It was very seldom we would agree on anything except "Transgression of the mind." We disagreed and argued so much, at one time, I thought he had gone blind in one eye, closed the other, and plugged his ears. Under no circumstances would he listen to reasoning from me—although he expected me to listen to him. We always had a difference of opinion. He and I were like the negative and positive wires in a light bulb; put them together and you have an explosion of light. That explosive light was like the vast radiance of the full blossoms of our friendship. My major question is, why did it take so many years for him to see the light of the point we argued so much about in prison? My philosophical approach with him always was: "You can catch more flies with sugar than you can with salt." I'd told him many times, "Let's not follow the white man's ways of evil, hatred, hypocrisy and deceitfulness. Let's find another way."

The Boston news media was well aware of Spike Lee's completion of his movie *Malcolm X*. It's a common practice that movie promoters begin publicizing their movie's opening date well in advance of the opening. This tactic is used to generate public interest and curiosity. After the movie premiere, they make millions on people satisfying their curiosity via their patronage. This approach demonstrates both a very good understanding of mass psychology, and good business sense, for in the movie industry it translates into profits.

My life over the years since my release from prison has been relatively simple and quiet. Occasionally, I've casually mentioned to a few people the fact that I knew Malcolm X personally. For years, it was completely ignored. Somewhere, somehow, it became public news that I was the character Shorty who Spike Lee was soon to be portraying in his upcoming movie. Suddenly those same people who ignored me for years were on my back like fleas on a dog in summer. All I can say is, "You bet your life…people are funny!"

The way I analyze that situation is everyone wants to be around a star; people feel that any affiliation with the motion picture industry will

Shorty playing with his very first band, after his release from prison with Malcolm X. *(left to right:* Herbie Lee, Joe Reddick, Willis Lee and Malcolm L. Jarvis.)

associate them with big money and the possibility of being on film. They think being close to anyone associated with the film industry will perhaps somehow glamorize their life. Out of a hundred, this may be true for a few, but not so in my case. Anyone who thinks along those lines has been grossly deceived and misled by their own thoughts. In the moviemaking business, some make money and others don't. I was one who didn't. However, money was not my concern when it came to anything pertaining to *Malcolm X*. This is more than I can say for some people who were closely associated with him during the making of the movie.

My association with Malcolm, post-prison, has always been spirituality-based, not monetarily-based. Even during the days when we were burglarizing homes, we did it more for excitement than for money. I was once falsely accused by someone close to him of selling him down the river for money. That symbolic shoe certainly doesn't fit me. An old Biblical saying comes to my mind: "Judge not, lest ye be judged."

People who, lacking the facts, quickly accuse others and are usually camouflaging either their own guilt or inadequacies, or covering their

Top: Shorty with Gail King of Channel 3 in Hartford, Connecticut. *Bottom:* Shorty in New York with Spike Lee.

Shorty in New York with Dan Rather.

own tracks. Need more be said? The accusation came about because I collaborated on a book about Malcolm. I did so out of the goodness of my heart and a deep, abiding respect for Malcolm X and all he advocated.

I was promised $500 and was never paid. The money was supposed to compensate me for my time invested. From the names I was called, you'd think I tried to rob the Brinks. I was called "a damn fool and an ass" by many of those "rubbernecks." Well, maybe I was, but my intentions were honorable. I believe, had Malcolm heard these words

Top: Shorty, prior to a speaking engagement in Springfield, Massachusetts (*left to right:* Brother Crocker, Pastor William Ford, Malcolm Lewis Jarvis, Jr., Malcolm Louis Jarvis, Sr., Pastor Amos L. Bailey and Paul Nichols). *Bottom:* Shorty playing with Tommy Simmons. A pianist and organist, the Tommy Simmons orchestra is very well known throughout Connecticut. The picture above was taken at Spat's Lounge in Groton, Connecticut (1987). Personnel are: Tommy Simmons, piano; Frank Wamsly, bass; Mal Jarvis, trumpet; Mike Sforza, drums; and Judd Watts, sax (not pictured).

Shorty with his grandson, Steven De Koenigswater (Clifford and Janka's child—and the famous Baroness' grandson).

spoken to me, he would have turned over in his grave. All the money circulating in his name: the movie, the books, the T-shirts, caps, etc.; and still, dissatisfaction due to greed. There is no happiness, because the more there is, the more there is to want. Regardless of what is said or thought about me, my claim to fame in my own eyes is honesty and sincerity from the depths of my heart concerning Malcolm X.

Each night I sleep with peace of mind, not aggravated or worrying over my bank book. I'll let the Supreme Power bear my witness to all, and be my Judge. In this case, my recollections are not for sale, and do not have a price tag which could be paid by anyone.

Another insight concerns Spike Lee, the director of the movie *Malcolm X*. Malcolm first met his wife in 1956, and married her in 1958. Before 1956, she did not exist in his life at all. Yet, she was the main consultant during production of the *Malcolm X* movie. Most of the things I mentioned in this book took place before 1956. I first met her in 1965, shortly after Malcolm's death. There are many things Malcolm never told Alex Haley during the writing of his book. I feel those things Malcolm never intended to become public news. I too shall respect Malcolm's wishes in this matter. Nonetheless, had I at least been contacted for a consultation, I could have contributed many interesting suggestions for the first half of the movie—in all probability, making it more interesting than it was. Whether or not Spike Lee was told I had expired, or simply thought I didn't exist, neither he, his company nor his crew ever made the attempt to verify their assumptions about me. Instead, he chose to play the part of my character as "Shorty" in the movie. The role he played (supposedly me) was utterly ridiculous, stupid and way out of character. It was not based on fact. He played me down a rat hole as long as the Brooklyn-Battery tunnel. Denzel Washington, on the other hand, should have won ten Academy Awards for his acting. I told the news media, "If Malcolm had lived, he couldn't have played the part any better himself." To Denzel, wherever you are, "You Were Terrific!"

Spike Lee found out about me too late. But he did have the decency to send me a couple tickets to the world premiere, and a copy of the movie, along with his wishes for me to enjoy it. For this, I Thank You, Spike.

I understand that Spike's next great undertaking (*The Jackie Robinson Story*) is in the works. Well Spike, I hope you redeem yourself with this film. It seems like that's in the cards. You're from Brooklyn: Jackie was a Brooklyn Dodger. Still, do your homework—don't make the same mistake twice. In my case, someone mislead you and it was really too bad. I hope you read this book and realize the contribution I could have made to the early episodes of the movie. I believe I could have offered a different perspective, a different point of view. All praise is due the Supreme Power. It was not meant to be.

8
The Vision

"The human or physical eye can be deceived
by optical illusions. The mind's eye sees through
deception, straight to the truth—if one would allow it.
Accuracy is derived from a confirmation of truth; and truth is to become
accurate with self. What you see and hear is not the deal. What you feel is
really real.
People like you according to what you think they are. For example; a
beautiful woman likes you for what you think she is.
Modern women fall into two categories: those who make a home for a man,
and those who make a man for a home.
In meeting a beautiful woman, I find myself being scared of her. I
experience and act upon an emotional contradiction: the feeling of inadequacy juxtaposed by the feeling of desirous wonder. If I really like
her, I act or say anything to indicate I have no interest. I won't dare look
her straight in the eyes, because I fear she might read me through and
through. My act is to be exceptionally polite without ignoring her. I
would never act or do anything to create a negative impression of any
kind. If the feeling is mutual, Mother Nature will play her part accordingly. If she is with another person, then my conversation is directed to
that person.
My sensation is not sexual, but purely aroused by the pleasure I derive
from the meeting.
It is in situations like this one that I am reminded of the power of
silence and non-action…For in this situation, silence is resounding…
Sight is soundless…speech is often inadequate… powerless…
If only people could understand, that far above the language of the human
tongue…abides the unspoken intercourse of hearts which truly understand—

without the necessity of speech. Silence...makes real conversation between friends. It's not in the saying, but in the never needing to say that counts.
—*By Malcolm "Shorty" Jarvis*

It's very strange how Malcolm always had a premonition of his death. Remembering our days of practicing mental telepathy and clairvoyance in the Charlestown prison gave me the impression we possessed both psychic tendencies and a telepathic connection. Being a musician all of my life, I recognized my emotional feelings were highly developed in many respects. Going through the mind transgression, which is the psychological process that results from the technique I've outlined earlier, gave birth to a mental compatibility between Malcolm and me. This harmonious mental relationship is what enabled me to see the death vision surrounding him the week before his death. Mind transgression has a tendency to incite intuition which people of the external world seldom see or experience.

A few weeks before his death, Malcolm suffered some bad disappointments which left him mentally off balance. Quiet as it's kept, his private life read like a scene from a horror comic strip. Malcolm X was a man-of-war, a thoroughbred—and he suffered the consequences. For example, on his last trip abroad, because he was considered an "undesirable," he was refused admission to France and was forced to return to England. Upon his return to this country, his house was bombed. Unbeknownst to the public at large, he was worried sick about his family's having a place to live. The daily phone threats on his life had escalated. He was very tired and in mental turmoil from all that was going on around him. This emotional onslaught was a lot for an old man, let alone a young man. These confusing problems aside, he still felt very uncomfortable reporting to the Audubon that fateful day. His now famous words concerning that engagement were, "I don't feel I should be here today." He was so right. His intuition was extremely strong.

On February 14, one week before the assassination, I was eating breakfast when I experienced a spiritual vision passing before me. It left me with a cold, damp chill. It came, I saw it clearly, and it left just as quickly. Instinctively, I said to my wife, "I must get in touch with Malcolm right away. Whatever he has planned for next Sunday he should cancel it, and bring his family to Connecticut to spend the day." As fate would have it, this vision was a death warning. I knew this because I had seen it a couple times before in my life. Each time I did, the person died within a week.

The first time I experienced this type of vision I was in the prison colony at Norfolk. Shortly thereafter, my first wife Hazel, the mother of my two children, died. The second time I experienced this type of vision I was still at Norfolk. It chronicled the death of my sister in 1949. I was nervous. The day "Sunday" came out of my mouth. Why I didn't say Thursday, Friday or Saturday, I don't know. All during that week I made several phone calls to the Theresa Hotel, Malcolm's headquarters at the time, and left messages for him to call me collect. I left my name and said it was urgent. I might as well have been waiting for Godot. I never heard a word from him. I had no way of knowing he was staying downtown at another hotel. For some reason, he didn't receive any calls or messages from the Theresa Hotel that week. All his correspondence was withheld, strangely.

Hearing nothing all week—which was peculiar unto itself, for no matter how big or how busy Malcolm got, he always found time to answer either my calls or my letters in a very timely fashion—I left Connecticut early Sunday morning to visit my relatives in Boston. At 3:05 P.M., a flash came across the TV, "Malcolm X has been assassinated."

The first words out of my mouth were, "Oh, no! If only he had received my messages and responded, he might still be alive."

Knowing of our intense spiritual relationship (similar to that attachment which twins often experience after birth) yet not doing more than to have phoned the hotel, I was sick at heart, then and now. That sick feeling in the pit of my stomach came as a result of my knowing how great his loss was to the world. I fear these feelings will never leave me.

Cecil B. DeMille didn't have anything on Malcolm. Malcolm X was "The Greatest Show on Earth!" Listen to him and tell me if you don't agree. For example, I firmly believe Malcolm was the only 20th century leader who could have personally turned today's young, black, street "gang-bangers" around—even the hardest of the hard core. Don't get me wrong, Louis Farrakhan is a powerful leader in his own right— I don't believe anyone else could have called over 1 million black men to Washington, D.C., on September 16, 1995, as Minister Farrakhan did. Although he could be thought of as a symbolically spreading oak tree, Minister Farrakhan is still greatly overshadowed by Malcolm X, who still stands in comparison as a sequoia, a redwood in the wilderness of life. Just look at and listen to the tapes of both and compare for yourself. Farakhan is still the student of Malcolm X.

8. The Vision

As I mentioned earlier, before going to prison, during our confinement, and after his release, Malcolm always had a premonition of a violent death. Often he said to me, "Everything I have ever done, I did by instinct to survive." This being the case, I wish I could understand why he went against his intuition and showed up at the Audubon on February 21, 1965. Had he had enough? Had he resigned himself to meet his fate, squarely? Only the Supreme Power knows.

Recently, I was reading the *Emerge* magazine's February 1995 issue. In it, there was an article entitled, "Malcolm X, His Final Days," by Mr. George E. Curry. It states that two days before his death, Malcolm met and had a conversation with the world famous photographer, Gordon Parks, of *Life Magazine*. The next day, he and his wife found a house they liked on Long Island, New York. Malcolm telephoned Alex Haley, who was crafting his *Autobiography*. He inquired about getting another advance from his publisher in order to move into the house.

The *Autobiography* states the first copyright was made in 1964, by Malcolm X and Alex Haley. If the book was completed in 1964, it had to have occurred a few months before his death: October, November or even December of 1964. Right after his death, in February of 1965, the book was re-copyrighted by his wife and Alex Haley. On the back cover of his book, Malcolm said, "I do not expect to live long enough to read my book." He also sensed and prophesied he would never see his 40th birthday. His prophecy was true. He neither lived to see his 40th birthday, nor did he ever read his *Autobiography* in its completed form.

Both the late Dr. Martin Luther King, Jr., and Malcolm X had a common intuition, or "mountain top" experience, before they passed on. Like looking through a glass, darkly, both saw their end and the end of their dreams. Both felt that if true brotherhood were to exist amongst people of all colors and nationalities, there would never be segregation. In this paradigm, inferiority or superiority complexes would not abound. People would be drawn together naturally, in spirituality. Malcolm felt this way upon returning from his Hajj, or pilgrimage to Mecca. The dream of Malcolm and Martin (both great black leaders) will, with hope, one day come true.

Being familiar with a skeptical public, I'm proud to announce many people can bear witness to the truth concerning my episodes—especially my ex-wife. For example, she was standing next to me on the fateful day I had the vision concerning Malcolm X's assassination. She was there when it was made manifest, and when it left. My prediction to her was, "Something is going to happen to Malcolm one week from today." Again, the Supreme Power knows that all that week I tried in vain to reach Malcolm. It was almost as if it were ordained that Malcolm X (a.k.a., "Detroit Red," who danced and cavorted his early life in ballrooms and "speakeasies") would "have his last dance" at the Audubon Ballroom, in shoes he would dye red with his blood.

I make no claims to fame, fortune or anything else. I realize I am not right about everything I think or do in life. I've made many mistakes and thought wrongly along the way. Not being infallible, I make no apologies. Through all and all, my ambition in life has been to remove my social blindfolds, seek understanding, and see the truth. Malcolm transgressed so far within himself, that he publicly prophesied the outcome of his life, predicting his own death. He told the world of his presence and foretold of his future demise through divine inspiration.

9
Extraordinary Phenomena

"Spiritual phenomena have an authenticity of great
significance. Investigation inspires their revelation of truth.
Even common knowledge is not born in us. It is acquired and cultivated by
being quiet... listening with all your senses...being fully present...

Understanding extraordinary phenomena takes an understanding of the power of awareness...of being present, and learning to listen dynamically when spoken to. The more I learn, the more I realize how little I know... If I knew, there would be no need to learn. I would be through and out the other end of this channel of life...I would be living in an exalted state of knowing...

Yesterday is behind me. I live in the present tense.
Tomorrow is not promised to me, although I try to look forward to
my future with enthusiasm.

In living today, I find myself trying to recapture yesterday.
In so doing, I find myself making myself miserable today.
Being miserable today, makes of me tomorrow, a sorry case to deal with.
I found out, I cannot recapture or relive the sadness of my past, my
yesterday, and expect to be happy today—and maybe tomorrow.
The learning: Don't suffer from the pain of the past.
Rather... live for happiness in the present...
To be happy in the future...be fully present in the present tense.

—*By Malcolm "Shorty" Jarvis*

Late in 1991, while in Connecticut, I received a phone call from Boston. To my surprise, it was two reporters from the *Boston Globe* newspaper requesting permission to visit me for a personal interview. They were Mr. Dan Golden and his photographer, Mr. Bill Cunningham. The next day, they drove 90 miles and spent the entire day extracting information from me about Malcolm X and my affiliation with him. On February 16, 1992, the entire "Magazine" section of the *Boston Globe* was about Malcolm X and his years in Boston. The article consisted of all the places Malcolm went, all the night clubs he frequented and the people he associated with. It was more or less about his life before going to prison. The appearance of this article occurred two months before our grave visit to both Malcolm X and Billie Holiday. It introduced and set the scene for the phenomenal spiritual events which would occur two months later.

The late Roy Wilkins, former executive secretary of the NAACP, said of the late Malcolm X, "He was a master spell binder. Even in death, he cast a spell far and wide—and more disturbing than he cast in life." And may I add on a positive note, it was his fearless heart that made him one of the most influential figures of this century.

April 10, 1992, I attended funeral services for Mrs. Gladys J. Cobb at the Abyssinian Baptist Church in New York City. She was both the daughter of my grandfather's sister, and first cousin to my mother. I will refer to her as Cousin Gladys. For better than fifty years, she was a devoted, faithful member of the Abyssinian Church.

She was born in Sea Bright, New Jersey. She departed this life on April 7, 1992. She was married to Mr. William F. Cobb of Danville, Virginia. He departed this life in 1957.

The Abyssinian Baptist Church was the church of the late U.S. senator Adam Clayton Powell and his father. While visiting the church, I was astounded at seeing the memorabilia honoring the late president John F. Kennedy and other distinguished members of the U.S. Senate and Congress. The archives were breathtaking in their splendor (some encased in glass) and all were donated to the church. The entire display was extremely interesting to me.

My cousin's most famous saying was, "If I can help somebody as I pass along this way, then my living will not be in vain." She was prepared for burial by the J. Foster Phillips Funeral Home. Through conversation with Mr. Phillips, the funeral director, I learned that Cousin Gladys' interment was to be conducted at the Ferncliff Cemetery in Hartsdale, New York. I said to Mr. Phillips, "Oh! that's where the late Malcolm X is buried. Do you know where?"

"No, but I will find out for you," he replied.

Mr. Phillips didn't have the slightest inkling of what my association with Malcolm X was—or whether I knew him at all. As the funeral procession entered Ferncliff Cemetery, a strange feeling came over me. In the silent worlds of my heart and mind, all I could feel and think about was how badly I wanted to visit Malcolm's gravesite while I was there.

After the church service for my cousin, my mind was not on her funeral. I felt from within, I had to see Malcolm mentally and visit with him, spiritually. I thought I could achieve this goal only at his grave. Standing at my cousin's grave, my mind floated away again, until I heard the minister say, "Ashes to ashes, and dust to dust."

Strange as it may sound, that emotional feeling of wanting to commune with Malcolm X was very strong in me. At this point, they were lowering my cousin's coffin into the sarcophagus when the undertaker spoke to me. I knew I wanted desperately to find the grave, but I had no great expectations, and to my surprise he said, "Mr. Jarvis, you inquired about the grave of Malcolm X. My associate informs me his grave is right behind you, about fifteen feet over there near the tree."

I thought to myself, "In such a large cemetery, how coincidental and strange this was: the mental alertness, the spiritual desire and my cousin's interment being so close to Malcolm's grave."

Originally, I had planned to go to the cemetery office to get the exact location. Mr. Phillips said, "You don't need to go to the office now." I felt that was so nice of him to go out of his way to find out the exact location for me. My friend, who had accompanied me from Boston for the service, walked over to Malcolm's gravesite with me. Knowing how I felt, she took a few steps backwards to give me a little privacy. (Incidentally, she was a professional jazz singer and her idol is the famous jazz and blues singer, Billie Holiday—better known as "Lady Day.")

The bronze plaque at the head of the grave read, "EL HAJJ MALIK EL SHABAZZ, known as Malcolm X." I went down on my knees (eyes closed in deep concentration and meditation—as we did in our days of old). I put my right hand on the plaque. A peculiar feeling went through me again. For some reason, I knew that Malcolm knew I was there. To me, this was all too real, for I could feel it. Malcolm's voice seemed to echo through my mind, saying, "Jarvis, it's about time you visited me."

I didn't feel the necessity to speak. This communication was in spirit. As I remained prostrate, his voice sounded like he was speaking from the grave. It was so clear and vivid. He said, "Thanks for coming. Carry on as best you can."

Before standing up, I picked up three stones from the top of the grave, and took them home as memorabilia. To me, bringing the stones home was like bringing a part of Malcolm home with me. Although he was not there in person, I could feel his presence deeply, everywhere all about. I felt he knew I still had his best interest at heart. Indeed, I sincerely did, and still do to this day. He is a loved one. Regardless of what certain people may think, from the day we met, to Malcolm, I have always been a dedicated friend in need. However, the hand of fate cut short our friendship—in the flesh.

Malcolm had been deceased 27 years, and April 10, 1992, was the first time I paid my respects. I'm not amazed at the strong, emotional stirrings I felt after all those years. In thought, I experience them frequently. In the spirit realm, I believe, there is no such thing as time and space. Malcolm was a very heavily spiritually-endowed person. What we felt and thought cut through time and space, and was present at the grave. It was definitely a spiritual communication.

After my cousin's funeral and the paying of respects to Malcolm, while driving up the highway heading back to Boston, my female companion, Liz English asked me, "Would you mind if we stopped in the Bronx to visit the grave of Billie Holiday?"

"What cemetery is she in?" I asked.

"She's in Saint Raymond's Cemetery," Liz replied.

When we got there, a woman in the cemetery office gave us the exact location of the grave. Once there, my friend jumped out of the car and ran anxiously to the grave—like she couldn't get there fast enough. Her display was like an emotional bonfire, an explosion of feelings. She went down on her knees, hugging and kissing the huge tombstone and crying like her heart was broken.

As I approached the grave, that same deep feeling which I had just experienced at Malcolm's gravesite came over me again. Only this time, my emotions overflowed in the form of tears. I was crying empathetically. I could feel what Liz was feeling. Malcolm X knew Billie Holiday personally while she was alive. He told a brief story about his associations with her on pages 128 and 129 of his *Autobiography*. I was not fortunate enough to know her while she lived.

Standing at her grave on that clear, sunny and cloudless mid-afternoon day, I felt somehow she knew Liz and I were there. There was an overwhelming spiritual presence at the gravesite. I felt as though I had known Billie Holiday all my life—like a sister. All these deep-rooted emotional feelings between Liz and me felt, to me, like we had brought the spirit of Malcolm X over to Billie's grave. It appeared we four became united in spiritual ecstasy. These feelings were strong, very intense, and in a way, dominating. Suddenly, a huge black cloud formed over the entire cemetery. The cloud opened up. I thought the ocean had dropped down upon us. I ran to get—and quickly retrieved—an umbrella from the car. We stood under the umbrella in silent prayer for ten minutes. As we began our departure from the cemetery, the rain stopped as suddenly as it had started, and the sun came out as brightly as ever. Liz and I thought this was an extraordinary phenomenon. I have discussed this incident with Liz many times, as it left us with a vivid impression we'll never forget. To this day, a good many years later, I still cannot understand where that ominous cloud of water came from on such a bright, sunny day. Were Liz and I vacationing in the Caribbean Islands, in Hawaii, the South Pacific or somewhere else below the Equator, I could understand the thunderous sun shower. But we were in New York, and there were no clouds at all in the sky that day. We concluded it was an inexplicable act of nature, orchestrated by the Supreme Power.

Liz and Shorty.

Two weeks after these incidents, Liz and I attended a Sunday afternoon jazz session in New Hampshire. The club was Luka's Green House, located on Route 1, in Hampton Falls, New Hampshire. Paul Broadnax, the famous jazz pianist, was appearing with his trio. Liz and I were Paul's invited guests.

Paul introduced us to his guest jazz singer, a Miss Jean Jones. She was from Portsmouth, New Hampshire. Through conversation, the name of Billie Holiday came up. Coincidentally, both Miss Jones and Liz were ardent admirers of Billie Holiday. During the course of our conversation, I casually mentioned our visit to Billie's gravesite and produced a picture of Liz at her tombstone.

Miss Jones was very interested, declaring her profound love for Billie, her style of singing and her accomplishments.

"Will you get me a picture of her grave?" Miss Jones asked me.

I told her that within a couple weeks I had some business in New York. I promised I would revisit Billie's grave and bring her some nice pictures for her archives. Both the atmosphere and the very air in the club seemed permeated by Billie's presence. That strong feeling came upon me. Again, it felt like Billie Holiday was present, in spirit.

Miss Jones started to sing Billie's favorite song, "God Bless the Child." She hit me right in the pit of my stomach with that tune. It was like the cantata of the rose—it was supernatural. She didn't complete one full chorus before I felt spiritually overwhelmed by some superior force beyond my control. I couldn't sit down. I leapt from my seat, and yelled in a loud voice, "Oh my God! That's not Miss Jones singing. That's Billie Holiday."

I guess people in the club must have thought I was out of my mind. I wasn't. They didn't know what was going on. My friend and I both agreed: Miss Jones sounded exactly like Billie Holiday—almost as if Billie had reincarnated herself in the body of Miss Jones in order to sing her favorite song for us, and thereby to thank us for our recent spiritual communication at her gravesite.

I am proud to say, Liz, who is alive and well today, will bear witness to the truth of my stories. She was astounded. By no means can she deny what she saw, heard and felt. It has been said, "What you feel is real." Strange as it may be, I had never heard Billie Holiday sing in person while she was alive, only on records. Yet, at that moment, I felt I had.

I made the trip to Saint Raymond's Cemetery again and took pictures, as promised. A month later, Liz and I returned to the club to present Miss Jones with the pictures. Her sister, Miss Sharon Jones, greeted us instead, informing us that her sister, Jean, had passed away. This news put Liz and me into a mild state of shock.

May the Supreme Power allow the soul of Miss Jean Jones to rest in eternal peace. For on that enchanted evening, she made me feel I had known Billie Holiday not only for one day but for a lifetime.

10
Dreams

> We may dwell in our dream world, but we'll never conquer it—especially if we're blinded, like so many of today's young "Gangsta Rappers," by the vacuous nothingness of wanton, existential anger. (Mathematically, nothing from nothing equals nothing. Even Einstein couldn't extract something from nothing.) Anger blinds real, dynamic vision—which is the precursor to real, dynamic action. Too many of us are either too blinded or too dishonest to see our anger.
> Honesty often makes me feel stupid—and humble.
> The reason for this feeling is: I see so little of it in people.
> True spiritual conversation consists of building upon another person's statements and observations, not overpowering or over-analyzing them. I love to hear people speak about themselves because I never listen to anything but that which is good. It helps me to see myself in the reflection of their goodness.
>
> *—Malcolm "Shorty" Jarvis*

Reminiscing on my spiritual experiences over the course of my life, I feel I understand more than words can explain. I have come to find that in an ultimate sense, no one really knows anything. Like the Ecclesiastical author, I have come to believe nothing makes any real sense. Life is fair and unfair, good and bad. For example, many black people have come to realize too late that Malcolm X was one of our most dedicated leaders; yet, he was gunned down by one of us like a thug in the streets. On the other hand, Charles Manson (still a celebrity sojourning behind bars) is living to a ripe old age. The more we learn, the more we know how much we need to learn. Again, in a real sense, we are at a loss to understand life's true meaning. But if we have a focus on a spiritually higher power, and from our relationship with that source, derive some sort of direction or develop a spiritual compass by which we can navigate and be guided to make the best choices for our lives, then we have a hold on life and can make of life what we will.

Many times in life we have been told, "If you want something badly enough, wish hard and it will come to you." This counsel is very true. It has happened to me many times—I've reflected on a couple of my experiences, earlier. It all depends upon the depth of one's beliefs and sincerity when one makes that wish. It does not work the way most people think. You will not receive what you want when you mentally demand or desire it; however, in the time of the Supreme Power, you will receive your heart's desires. What you wish for is often received in an unpredictable and illogical way—nature is totally logical and illogical all at the same time.

Both the brain and mind, in this enigma of life, have the fluid capacity to adjust to life; yet, in their ability to function on such visceral and spontaneous levels, they are lacking. There are so many life experiences we cannot use our brains to understand. In my opinion, the human brain is little more than an electrodynamic, cellular oscillator, capable of producing an electric alternating current with an indeterminable level of output. Both this uncertainty and the relatively static functioning of the brain makes it an unpredictable and indefinite transmitter and receiver. Ultimately, it is a faulty tool, but it is all with which we have to work.

As you have seen, I have always been aware of the presence of unexplained phenomena in my life from an early age. I have always been extremely humbled by their occurrence. They are like an Australian aboriginal "dream time" phenomenon which we experience in our awakened state. They are like mini-dreams which, if we can but discover their origin, can bring us to the fountainhead of personal power. For example, I want to know how we can get lost in the stars dreaming or thinking strongly about someone far away, and later have them tell us, "I thought about you, today?" I would like to know how inexplicable events like that take place: the cause, the reason and the effects. Nothing happens in this world without a reason, and every reason has its cause and its effect. Likewise, I believe the only way a person can read another's mind is through some form of mental telepathy. There are people who can meet you for the first time and possess the ability to read and to analyze you like a book—without the necessity of speech. With these people, when you open your mouth to speak, you confirm their convictions and either condemn or honor yourself. (It would be nice if people would remember that first impressions are lasting ones.)

Dreams have a power we must learn to harness. We should not let them escape as we awaken only to get sucked up in the vortex, the turbulent waters of our lives in the external world. We should record, study and analyze our dreams to reach our own interpretations, for no other interpretation of our dreams for us is as good as our own. After all, no one else walks in our moccasins but us. We must be the ultimate authority of our own dreams.

The first interpretations of a dream and its symbolic meanings should come from the emotional feeling one receives in the pit of one's stomach. Sometimes dreams alert us to our purpose and the possibilities which exist beyond ego in our awakened state. Dreams take us beyond the limits or boundaries which are imposed upon us by others and ourselves. Dreams reveal to us aspects of ourselves we may have denied or may have suppressed. Through dreams, we can recognize our denials, even our guilt, and ultimately make peace with ourselves. In recalling dreams, we glimpse events considered at once both trivial and momentous—before they occur. It's believed that dreams are triggered by sufficient, long and thorough meditation. The world's creativity comes through dreams. In addition to being an avenue to the subconscious mind, dreaming is also the throughway to the human soul. If through our souls we are likened unto God, then our dreams are yet another vehicle wherein we can experience God.

Earlier, I remarked about how I used to do nothing else but daydream during my incarceration with Malcolm X. There, I learned to live with my dreams. Developing and understanding that process has taken its effect upon me. Over the years, I have found dreams to be an immense source of inner strength and spiritual guidance.

Through dreams, mankind has searched for clues to the purpose, the meaning, and the destination of the soul. From his primeval soul searching efforts, man has come close to the answer, but has never quite found it completely. Man is now drifting toward the other extreme, where he discourages—in a tacit way—any such mental and spiritual inner exploration. Not exploring our more spiritual natures is a bad thing, for the emptiness that afflicts our society is related to the fact that, in general, we are grossly out of touch with our inner natures, our inner lives, our more spiritual selves.

In 1933, eminent psychologists and psychiatrists from some of the most prominent universities performed experimental, extrasensory perception tests on 20 students from the Julliard School of Music. The results were amazing. The musicians scored remarkably high. It was recognized that students with creative abilities were more susceptible to extrasensory phenomena than anyone else. Perhaps this result occurred because their creative abilities stemmed from their highly overdeveloped emotional inner lives. I am convinced that mental telepathy, clairvoyance, extrasensory perception and dreams have an uncanny, inexplicable relationship.

Lastly, by no means do I possess a degree in anything on the subjects about which I have written—beyond living 75 years in the 20th Century. I am but a pebble in the mountains of time. Yet, my episodes are true experiences which took place during my lifetime. I have shared my thoughts and told these stories to the best of my ability in hopes that others may learn and benefit from them. With that, I say thanks for taking the time to discover the truth. May you and your dreams be kept in the hollow of our Supreme Power's hand.

Afterword
by Paul D. Nichols

Of all the immensely challenging things that I have done to date, writing this book has made its place at the top of the list. Although working with "Shorty" was a fascinating experience (he was very intelligent, well-spoken, and complex—and he played a "mean" trumpet) that alone could not diminish the intensity of working through all aspects of bringing this book to fruition.

Yet, it was an honor to have had the privilege of working through this rugged challenge—which persisted even after I had completed the final manuscript. But it did not begin there.

Hearing Shorty's message, initially, made me a bit leery about taking on this project. First and foremost, I had to get past the phrase "transgression of the mind." That took all of one and a half years—despite the fact that Shorty told me the word came to him as a clear, spiritual revelation.

In the final analysis, it was Shorty's passionate conviction in relating that this phrase came to him one day as a divine inspiration that allowed me to uncoil my back and write Shorty's book, using his ideas—as he would have them phrased.

Then, I had to get past Shorty's justified comments about his portrayal in the book, *The Autobiography of Malcolm X*. On the one hand, I was torn because it was Shorty's life Alex Haley was talking about, and the facts about Shorty's life, as stated in the book, simply were not true. Anyone would be upset at the portrayal. But, on the other hand, George Haley, Alex's attorney brother, is a personal friend who'd indirectly helped me as a 23-year-old by walking my executive director, Earl Fitzhugh (and thereby, me), through the establishment of a corporation in the late 1970s—at the height of his brother Alex's fame (that tells you what kind of guy George is). His painstaking precision, effort, time and breadth of knowledge about corporate law was truly impressive and immeasurably helpful. Remembering what George had done for us made it extremely difficult to abide such open criticism of Alex, his brother, who I'd considered nothing less than a great writer and role model.

What's more, during the writing of this book, my first cousin, Cathy, had married Minister Farrakhan's nephew, Joel. (Although I respect deeply the honorable Minister Farrakhan, I do not accept all that he says.) Shorty's comments made me feel uneasy.

Lastly, I think that as a person of a different generation and upbringing, I found Shorty's message (in particular, his racial comments and certain of his spiritual beliefs) somewhat jarring and otherwise difficult to accept fully.

I was a child of the sixties. I marched in the streets (with a "rainbow" of people). I had hope then, a hope that, "we shall overcome"—ourselves or anything else to survive and ultimately succeed as a people. It is a hope that I have not abandoned. (As a footnote, I must add, I abandoned my allegiance to the peace movement when it turned sour. When it became "hawkish" about the dove of peace, castigating and otherwise disowning those very brave young men—some of whom were in my "rainbow" of friends and family—who went to Vietnam to ensure the "self-determination" of the Vietnamese people. Muhammad Ali said it best, "In this country [the black soldiers'] own civil rights were being denied them." It took a special person—a true hero—to handle the "fallout." Besides, I was not raised that way. I was raised to believe loyalty is the breastplate of brotherhood.)

Also, I grew up in a strong, Christian household (Surprisingly, I could handle Shorty's comments about Christianity—I guess. The institution has taken worse hits over the years.) in an ethnically diverse neighborhood, in a working class section of Cambridge, Massachusetts. Irish, WASP, Italian, Greek, Armenian, Dutch, German, Southern Black, West Indian Black, Jewish, Asian, Lithuanian—all I would interact with, and all floated in and out of my childhood on a weekly basis. Of all those individuals representing the cultures listed above, all I considered my friends and most nearly all I found to be sympathetic to the causes of the civil rights movement then underway in this country.

Shorty relaxing prior to a speaking engagement (1989).

I credit my father with instilling in all 11 of his children the value of Christian love (I am a Christian). I credit my mother with coaching us throughout our upbringing, through the understanding of this value and facilitating the practical application of this Christian love in our lives (with all its many ramifications). As a result of my upbringing in the culturally-diverse environment in which I grew up, I, for one, have come to realize there is strength in diversity. I have come to see—like the Rastafarian view purports—that we are "one" in humanity, one in love.

In fact, my viewpoint is borne out in the diversity represented in the "rainbow" of ethnicities evident in the marriages of my sisters, brothers and me (Asian, African, Southern Black, Cape Verdean, Native

American, Irish, Spanish, and West Indian–Jamaican), and *all* are welcomed additions to our loving family. I think my parents did a wonderful job of encouraging us to broaden our outlooks on people as individuals (and groups), and this focus, I believe, has helped us to broaden our outlook on life itself.

These were my "crosses to bear" in making the decision to edit this book. Nonetheless, Shorty and I agreed on my reviewing the first three chapters of the book before making a final commitment. I knew that commitment would challenge my ability to remain objective under fire, as Shorty's perspectives on race and spirituality are far different from mine. Yet, he was entitled to his opinions as was I to mine, and I must say, with mutual accord, we gave each other's opinions and viewpoints respect throughout the duration of this project. In this regard (as well as many others), Shorty was a "class act."

When Shorty called to inform me that he had sent me the first three chapters of his manuscript, I found I could hardly wait to receive them. (He said this, his final book, took 25 years to write—most of that time going into research—and that it was a total of 104 double-spaced, typewritten pages—the finished product was 280 double-spaced, typewritten pages.) It was at that moment of waiting impatiently that I'd realized how historical a project this one was going to be. What registered most at that time was who Shorty was, in an historical context. His place in history transcended my personal issues. I had all but made my decision.

The day Shorty's first three chapters arrived, I was beside myself with excitement. I realized, for the first time, I was touching history. Upon reading these chapters, I felt their power immediately. I got up and cleaned my entire house. They were so powerful! Their power belied the fact that their author was a man whose education had been short-circuited prior to his completing high school. It was a visceral wakeup call. I knew in my gut this book was going to be about the message, not the messenger.

At the time (and still to this day), I found the message, in many ways, prophetic, and therefore far greater than me. I made my decision. I then chose to push my personal feelings aside and decided to edit the 104 pages, which constituted Shorty's greatest life work. Again, it was quite an honor then and an honor now to have been considered for this job.

My challenge in writing this book was to tell the story as Shorty would have it told in his own words—with words Shorty would have used. In the original manuscript, the language was extremely compact, so condensed that often Shorty and I would have to engage in conversations over several days to get to the essence of his message—that, in itself, to me was testament to the depth of this man. Upon getting to the gist of what he was trying to say, often I found myself engaged in extensive research.

The number of Shorty's books which he suggested I read, and the many videotapes of his which I watched, would take up several pages of space in any bibliography. We have tried to make this a different type of book, though. We wanted this book to be informal and anecdotal. We engaged in the research not to overshadow the message with facts and figures, but in order to render perspective to the message. No extensive quotes were taken from these books or tapes. (For instance, in reference to the word "transgression;" after hours and days of discussion, research and more discussion, our research would culminate in a full day trip to both the Hartford and New London main branches of the public libraries, pouring through their largest dictionaries, etymologies and thesauruses. It would also include scrounges through their linguistics sections while in hot debate the entire time. Dr. West would get involved with the debate briefly, and later suggested we consult Paul Tillich.) Ultimately, I think we have arrived at a manuscript which represents well the man, his ideas and his message in his own conversational tone. (It should be clear that this book is Shorty's. These are his ideas. I merely have put them together in a way that the reader can digest them.)

Two days before Shorty passed, I spent ten hours at his home and completed this project. He wished me the best on this project, assuring me he knew it was "in good hands" (even though he did not know how often I'd felt humbled by the scope and dimension of the project and the ideas contained therein). That day, upon leaving, strangely, Shorty, looking through me to a far off, distant place, said, "Good-bye." (I found it so disturbing, I spoke to his wife, Liz. For, prior to that time, Shorty would always say something like, "When do you think you'll be back, Paul?" I could not help thinking about the many discussions I had had with Shorty concerning premonitions and extraordinary phenomena. "He knows he doesn't have much time, now. He means it. He was telling you, 'good-bye,' Nichols," Liz told me.)

One and a-half days later, Shorty was gone. I trust his words will live on.

As concerns references made to Malcolm X in this book, from the outset, we endeavored to write *Shorty's* story. Malcolm X's story has been told to the satisfaction of his family. We had chosen not to mention much more about Malcolm X unless it were to shed some new light on the man. In other words, in a commercially-driven venture, an expectation or tendency with such a story would preclude getting caught up in a commercially-motivated emphasis on Malcolm X—at the expense of Shorty. Through all aspects of this story, we focused on Shorty. Malcolm X is mentioned in relation to Shorty, not vice-versa. As a result, this book represents an humble attempt at presenting Shorty's vision, the vision of a "seer," (a daunting task), and interpreting this vision in a way that the reader can experience it. (In fact, that term "seer" in reference to Shorty was first coined by Dr. Cornel R. West after he'd just spent five hours in a videotaped interview with Shorty. Both the cameraman at that meeting, Mr. Cruz Sanabria, and an attorney who was present, Mr. Joel R. Davidson, endorsed Dr. West's feelings.) Often, with this interpretation, I had found myself amidst an internal battle over whether or not Shorty's words would come across—above and beyond my words. It was at these times that I was reminded of truth, which, like a mountain, has the power, the living force, to transcend the words we use to describe it. Once that reminder came from Dr. West, when he inferred through his experience with Shorty that Shorty's words had the power to transcend themselves and to take on an air of prophecy, I could let go (and let truth).

Speaking of mountains, alas, it is fitting that I should have finished this book on the Skyline Trail in the magical and energy-filled Mt. Ranier National Park. The depths of mystery and profound thought into which I have plunged are equal, symbolically, to the sublime heights and primeval power of this majestic, West Coast monument. Here, on this clear day, my newlywed wife and I saw one heart-shaped cloud about halfway up the peak of the mountain which appeared motionless, caressing the mountain—until it was blown apart, and absorbed by the misty majesty of the mountain and its ever-present, powerful, weather-making winds.

Spiritual, New Age mysticism? Honeymoon romance? Optical illusion? That is how I would have characterized the experience above, before meeting and working with Shorty. Over the past two and a half years (and up to two days before his death) I have bridged a spiritual divide. In my spirit, I have "moved to the mountains." It is as the Taos

Pueblo Indian says in his poem, "I Went To Kill the Deer," "The heart of the mountain beats for those who live there."

Since I was a child and read *The Autobiography of Malcolm X*, I had been intrigued with who this man "Shorty" was, and why we had not heard anything about him. I remember wondering if he continued his prison studies and eventually reinvented himself, or if he reverted to his preprison ways and inevitably was consumed by the streets, like so many others. (I wondered also if what they studied in prison and the intensity with which they studied was comparable to a college or graduate degree. If what Shorty put me through in the two and a half years I had worked with him is any indication of the level of study that Malcolm X and he were on while in prison, then their studies were at the Ph.D. level and beyond. Also, upon meeting Shorty, I wanted to know how they were able to change so radically. To my knowledge, this is the first time either of them has attempted to document specifically their process of change. I trust in our humble attempt at explaining Shorty's "transgression of the mind" theory we have been able to shed some light. (Shorty had mentioned that in some "B" movie this theory is used as a motif, but I have not been able to find it.) Never would I have guessed that I would be working with "The Shorty" so closely, on such an important, historical document. For, in spite of what we might think of the man or his message, what stand are his life, his story, and his experiences. They are true. They speak volumes about what previously has been mere innuendo and, ultimately, fictionalizations. For if we were to believe the books or movie, we would have no option but to believe Shorty, as he says, "a buffoon." He has been miscast in the national media script—and often much to the financial gain of his presenters. (Shorty, on the other hand, to his dying day, vowed never to participate in the exploitation of Malcolm X's name.) He deserves to have the record set straight, for posterity, because it is just right, because you have read his words and now know these are not the words of a "buffoon." I trust that after reading this book you walk away seeing the true depth of this man. Like my dear friend, Dr. West, I too believe him a "seer," of sorts. For Shorty to have been so far on the wrong side of the law, to walk so far (approximately 55 years) on the "right" side of reformation, he had to have seen something.

Yet, many who know Shorty say he was not a civil rights advocate, leader, etc. They say he scattered his energies, for example—marrying four times in the process. "How can you listen to a 'messenger' who

Paul D. Nichols and Cornel R. West after Paul's wedding at Pond Street Baptist Church, Providence.

conducts himself like that?" they ask. I argue, forget the messenger. Listen to his message. What was he saying? Does it strike a chord? Is there something here that enriches you?, something here with which you can walk away?

In fact, when I think of messengers, the image that comes to mind is that of the battlefront of long ago—well before the proliferation of technology. I see war-torn infantrymen in desperate need of a word from "The Front." I see a messenger dispatched. When these infantrymen were dispatched with messages of vital importance to troops beyond the communication loop often miles away, upon arrival, I would bet the awaiting troops in those survival-challenging times would cut the dead weight concerning the messenger's appearance. I am sure no one would waste valuable time criticizing the messenger for unpolished buttons or boots—their concern would be with the message.

Aren't we at war in the streets of our inner cities? Aren't we searching desperately for a message from someone to help in saving the lives of our youth? Yes, these are serious, survival-challenging times. And Shorty's is a prison message of sorts to our youth—parts of the book are like a warning to them from prison; it is relevant to those of our youth who are suffering from their self-imposed, physical and mental bondage, living, as Shorty said, "the life of extroverts," without taking the time to reflect deeply, on who they are or what they are becoming.

Like Shorty thought about Malcolm X, I think about Shorty, for I have seen it with my own eyes. I think Shorty, if only he would have lived, could have contributed greatly in galvanizing many of this country's youth to (as he and Malcolm X did) turn their lives around. Again, I saw his effect on students at the Dearborn Middle School, Cambridge Rindge and Latin High School and Hyde Park High School. In fact, I think that if you really read his book, you will hear a resounding message to our youth: "Check out your mind. You have the power to change." (Ultimately, if you read it in tandem with the *Autobiography*, I think you will hear a rather profound message from both men—and in the process, fill in some gaps and correct some inconsistencies about each of their lives.)

It is most unfortunate that all we are left with now are his words, many of which, for some, strike discordant chords; but the overall theme, or medley of his words is all about self-development as individuals and as a peoples. I trust we will, in a positive way, forget the dissonant appearance (and chords) of the messenger and hear the truth-filled assonance of his message.

Index

Absolute Being 112
Abyssinian Baptist Church 144
Affirmative Action 7
Africa 110, 113, 114, 117–119, 121
African Cosmological View 119, 120
African Culture 122, 123
African Population 121
African Religion 70, 71, 107, 117–123
African-American Males 68
African-Americans 119, 122
Africans 107, 110, 118–122
Ahmad, Mirza Ghulam 125
Ahmadiyyas, Ahmadiyyan 56, 125, 126
Albino 89
Alcohol 87, 109
All and All 95
Allah 9, 10, 90
All-Good 112
All-in-All 69
All-Knowing 112
All-Powerful 112
Almighty 69
America 61, 75, 114
American Federation of Musicians 24
Amsterdam News 13
Amtrack 39
Amun 120
Ancestors 119, 122
Anderson, Cat 30
Arabic 57, 125

Arabs 107
Armstrong, Louis 30
Army (United States) 20
Arrest 53
"A-Tisket, A-Tasket" 30
Audubon Ballroom 139, 141, 142
Australia 77
The Autobiography of Malcolm X 8, 108, 125, 141, 146
Ayatollah 71

Babalawos 120
Barnett, Charlie 30
Basie, Count 30
"The Bastille Concerto" 8
Bazarian, Beatrice 44–46, 49, 50, 65
Bebop 98
Bible 16, 58, 61, 68, 72, 86–88, 90, 102, 117, 118
"Bird" 98
Black History Month 122
Black Man 12, 60, 88–91, 93, 107–111, 113, 114, 117, 120
Blacklisting 28
Body and Soul 56
Bonito, Dorothy 17
Booker, Joe 42
Boston, MA 15, 24–28, 35, 39, 43, 48, 49, 51, 56, 95, 125, 126, 140, 143, 144, 146
Boston Daily Record 64
Boston English High School 24

The Boston Globe 22, 23, 143, 144
Boston University 17
Boston University Extension School 8
Boxing 39
Boy Scout 24
Breaking and Entering 53, 63
Brewsters 17
Britain 118
Britannia 118
Broadnax, Paul 148
Bronx 146
Brooklyn, New York 137
Brooklyn Dodger 137
Buddhism 70, 107
Bussing 27
Buttrick, The Honorable Allen G. 61, 64, 67, 111

Cabrini, Frances X. 79
Caines, Brian 42
Caines, Eugene 42
Calloway, Cab 30, 33
Cambridge, MA 53, 54, 108
Candomble 120
Canton, MA 24
Carlton, Jack 31
Carter, William E. Post No. 16 21
Caucasian 88
Cayuga 15
Charles River 53
Charlestown Prison 125, 139
Cherry Hill 104
Chicago 13, 126
Chinese 107
Christianity 11, 55, 58, 61, 72, 101, 107–109, 114, 117, 121, 122, 123
Christians, Techno/Nuclear Age 70
Churchill, Winston 63
Civil Rights 7
Claus, Fred 64
Club Dixie 26
Club La Marr-Cheri 48
Cobb, Gladys J. 144
Cobb, William F. 144
Collins, Ella 64, 126, 130
Columbus Avenue 25, 44
Condon Street 38
Conking 34
Connecticut 139, 140, 143
Connor, Bull 71

Conrail 21
"Cool Jazz" 98
Cosmology 120, 121
Cradle of Civilization 118
Creator 69, 112, 122
Crusades 118
Cunningham, Bill 23, 144
Curry, George E. 141

D. A. 53, 62, 63
Dale Street (#72) 33, 65
Dali Lama 71, 75, 76
Damballah 77
Danville, Virginia 144
Darwish, Mahmud 98
Davis, Miles 98
Deputy Warden 126–128
Detroit 33
"Detroit Red" 34, 36, 42–44
Devil 111, 112, 123
"Devil's Brew" 109
Dizzy 98
Dorsey, "Big Bill" 42
Dover Street 56
Dreams 77, 151–153
Dream-time 77, 151
Dudley Street 51, 52
Duke, David 71

East 113, 118
East Coast 13
Eckstine, Billy 30
Edgecomb Avenue 47, 48
Egypt 55, 56, 110, 118, 120
Einstein, Albert 71
Eisenhower, Dwight D. 15
Ellington, Duke 30
Emerge magazine 141
Encyclopedia of Mammals 87, 88
"Ending of the Christian Era" (article) 114–117
England 17, 118, 139
English, Liz 146–149
Equal Opportunity 7
Establishment 109
Estelle's Lounge 25
Ethiopian 89, 107
Etymology 88
Euro-Centric 118
Europe 88, 120

"Everything Contained Within
  Everything" 69
"Everything That Happens Praise Ye
  the Lord" 122
Evil 112, 113, 120

Fard, W. D. 11
Farrakhan, Minister Louis 140
Father 86
Federal Revenue Act 28
Ferguson, Leroy 97
Ferncliffe Cemetery 144, 145
Fertile Crescent 118
The Final Call 13
Fireside Chats 28
First World 121
Fitzgerald, Ella 30
Fogey's Barber Shop 8
"The 400 Group" 33
France 139
Franklin Park 39
Freud, Sigmund 75–77
*Funk & Wagnalls Standard College
  Dictionary* 89
Funkadelik 101

Gambling House 50
Garagulian, Joyce 44, 65
Genet, Jean 66
Germany 28
Ghandi 68, 108
Glycerin 30
God 61, 65–67, 72, 80, 86, 101, 103, 111,
  112, 117, 119, 120, 122, 123, 152
"God Bless the Child" 148
Golden, Dan 23, 144
Gone with the Wind 31
Good 112, 113, 120
Graham, Billy 122
Grzimek, Bernard 87, 88
Guardian Angel 54
Gun(s) 42, 50–53

Haiti 77, 119
Hajj 130, 141
Haley, Alex 117, 123, 136, 141
Hameed, Abdul 55, 58, 125, 126, 128,
  129
Hammond, Masson 55
Hammond Street 55

Hammurabi 117
Hampton, Lionel 30
Hampton Falls, New Hampshire 148
Hannibal 117
Hartsdale, New York 144
Hawkins, Coleman 56
Heaven 102, 111
Heliotropic Myth 118
Hell 90, 102, 108, 111
Henderson, Fletcher 30
"Hi-De, Hi-De, Hi-De, Ho!" 33
Highest God 118, 123
Hi-Hat Club 25, 44
Hindu 68
Hinduism 70
Hiram of Abiff 108, 110
Hitler, Adolf 54
Hodges, Bruds 18
Hodges, Johnny 30
The Hole 126, 128
Holiest of Holies 66
Hollander Street 33, 46, 52
Holliday, Billie 22, 23, 144–149
Holt, George 50, 51
Holy Bible 54
Holy City 130
Holy Ghost 122
Holy Grail 110
Holy Land 130
Holy Scriptures 112, 118, 130
Homeric Mythology 117
Hoover, J. Edgar 71
Houghton's Pond 20, 24
Houngan 119
House Committee on Un-American
  Activities 28
Humboldt Avenue 33
Hunter, Ivory Joe 30
Hussein, Saddam 71

Ifa Tradition 120
Iman 126
Incarceration 65, 66
India 55, 125, 126
Indians, North American 15
Irish, Barbara 17
Iron Curtain 63
Iroquoian-Caddoan 15
Iroquois Indians 15
Isaiah 66:17 88

Iscariot, Judas 58
Islam 55, 70, 107, 121, 124, 125, 129
Italian Facists 28

"J. C." 31
The Jackie Robinson Story 137
Japanese Imperialism 28
Jarvis, Clifford, Jr. 18, 20, 24
Jarvis, Clifford Osbourn 14, 15, 18, 22
Jarvis, Donald 18, 20
Jarvis, Elsie 18
Jarvis, Ethel 22
Jarvis, Herbert 18
Jarvis, Malcolm L. 15, 22, 23, 38, 64
Jarvis, Rufus 21
Jarvis, Theodore 21
Jarvis, Vera 21
Jazz 25–28, 30, 31
Jesus Christ 11, 16, 54, 55, 58, 61, 71, 107, 110, 118, 123
Jewish 107
Jews 54, 109
John 2:15–17 86
Johnson, John 64, 66
Jones, Jean 148, 149
Jones, Sharon 149
Judaeo-Christian Tradition 117, 123
Judaism 107, 118
Julliard School of Music 153

Kadahfi 71
Kennedy, John Fitzgerald 22, 144
Kenton, Stan 30
King, Donald 21
King, Dr. Martin Luther, Jr. 17, 68, 108, 110, 141
King, Priscilla 23
King James 54, 118, 122
King Solomon 117
Kitt, Ertha 28
Korea 67
Korean War 21
Ku Klux Klan 108
Kwanzaa 119

"Lady Day" 145
Laura 12
Lee, Herby 25
Lee, Spike 12, 131, 136, 137
Letter (Mother's) 70

Leviticus 11: 7 88; 11:3 87
Lewis, Sabby 42
Life magazine 141
Lincoln, Abby 30
Lincoln, Abraham 7, 109
Liston, Melba 30
Little, Malcolm 7–13, 31, 33, 34–42, 44–56, 58, 61, 62, 64, 65, 70, 87, 97, 108, 110, 111, 113, 125–132, 134, 136, 137, 139, 141, 144
Little, Reginald 10, 11, 125
Little Harlem 26
Little Rock, Arkansas 27
Local 535 24
Long Island 141
Longine Wristwatch 36–38
The Lord 88
Los Angeles 13, 44
The Los Angeles Dispatch 13
Luka's Green House 148

Madison Avenue 37
Maine 17
Malcolm X 7–9, 12, 13, 17, 18, 22–24, 26, 31, 39, 58, 66, 68–70, 72, 76, 79, 82, 87, 95–98, 103, 108, 110, 118, 124, 125, 129, 131, 132, 134, 136, 139, 140, 141, 142, 144–147, 150, 152
"Malcolm X, His Final Days" (article) 141
Manson, Charles 150
Marderosian, Cora 44, 46, 65
Masons (Masonic) 17
Massachusetts, Framingham 52
Massachusetts, Plymouth 17
Massachusetts Avenue 25, 26, 40, 42, 44
Mattapan, MA 16
Mayflower 17
McCarthy, Senator Joseph 71
McDaniel, Hattie 31
McElroy, Clarence 64
McGovain, Johnny 50, 51, 55, 70
McNight, Sammy 46–48
Mecca 130, 141
Medicine Man 75
The Messenger 9
Metropolitan Theatre 26
Michigan 8
"Middle Passage" 107

Middlesex County Jailhouse 53, 54
Middlesex Superior Court 64
Milky Way 63
Miller, Glenn 31
Mohawks 15
Morgan, Al 42
Morrison, Carol 17
Morrison, Connie 17
Morrison, David 17
Morrison, J. Clair 17
Morrison, Louis 17
Morrison, Louis, Jr. 17, 18
Morrison, Margie 17
Morrison, Peter 17
Morrison, Phillip 17, 18
Morrison, Sharon 17
Morrison, Virginia 17
Mosby's Medical & Nursing Dictionary 87
Moslem 12, 121, 125
Mount Hope Cemetery 16
Muhammad 125
Muhammad, The Honorable Elijah 9–13, 56, 125, 126
Muhammad Speaks 13
Muslim, Ahmadiyyan 55
Muslim Mosque, Inc. 130
Muslims 126, 129
Myself & I 85, 86, 91–93

NAACP 144
Nance, Roy 30
Nation of Islam 9, 10, 13, 107, 125
The National Federation of Musicians 27, 28
Native American 119, 121
"Nature Mysticism" 121
Nazism 28
Near East 88
Negro(es) 88, 89, 93
New Delhi 68
New Hampshire 147
New Orleans 119
New World 123
New York City 13, 39, 46, 47, 148
Newport News, Virginia 15, 16
Nigger(s) 88, 89
The Nile Valley 118, 120
Norfolk Prison Colony 8, 18, 125, 129, 130, 140

Northern Hemisphere 114
Nubian Heiroglyphics 117
Nuremberg Trials 109

O'Neil, Charles 97
The Odd Fellows 17
Ogun 77
The Old Savoy Club 25, 42, 44, 49
One Supreme 112
Oneida 15
Onondagas 15

Pakistan 125
Parks, Gordon 141
Pawnshop(s) 51, 52
Peeping Tom 40
Phillips, J. Foster 144, 145
Phillips, J. Foster Funeral Home 144
Pilgrims 17
Pool 34–37
Pool Halls (Rooms) 34, 35, 37
Portsmouth, New Hampshire 148
Powell, Adam Clayton 144
Pratt, Ricky 42
Preserver of the Universe 112
President Roosevelt 28
Prince Hall Masonic Lodge 21
"The Prison Cell" 98
Prison Colony 78, 79, 110, 128
Punjab 125
Pygmalion 56
Pyramids 88

Racketeers 49
Rashee 56–58, 104
"Red" 34, 36, 48, 49, 51
Register, Hazel 22, 39, 40, 46, 140
Religion 108
Revelations 3:19 123
Righteousness Guides (Rules) 82
Rite of Kanzo 77
R.K.O. Boston Theatre 26
Roach, Max 27, 30
Robbins, Charles S. 64
Robinson, Jackie 137
Rock 'n' Roll 128
Rolex 36, 51
"Rout Kin in the Sentencing of 2" (article) 64

Route 1 148
Roxbury 15, 33, 38, 55, 62
Ruler 112
Russia 28

Sabby Lewis Orchestra 25, 42
Saint Nicholas Avenue 47, 48
Saint Raymond's Cemetery 146, 148
Saints 123
Sandwich Salesman 39, 52
Santeria 120
Satan 89, 90
Savior 11
Saxophone 7, 24
Sea Bright, New Jersey 144
Seneca 15
Shabazz, Attilah 22
Shabazz, Betty 22, 23, 136
Shabazz, El Hajj Malik El 145
Shaman 75
Shelbourne, Charles 21
Shelbourne, Claire 21
Shelbourne, Jackie 21
Shelbourne, Janice 21
Shelbourne, Johnny 21
Sherborn 65
Shorty 44, 46, 131, 136
Shubert Theatre 26
Shultz, Dutch 39, 46, 70
Silver (Dollars) 57, 58
Smallwood, Richard 122
Smith, Anna 20
Smith, James 20
Smith, Sam 20
Smith, Virginia 20
South Pole 95
Southern Hemisphere 114
Spanish Nationalists 28
Speakeasies 26
Spiritual Divining 118
Spratley, Lucy Ann 15, 16
Stanton, Dakota 30
State Prison at Charlestown 65
"Streetcorner Bone Men" 119
Strother, Gloria 12, 39
"Study of the Soul" 110
Sugar Hill 33
Supreme Being 81
Supreme Power 10, 15, 16, 20, 22, 66, 69, 95, 131, 136, 137, 141, 142, 147, 149, 153
Syndicate 46

Tasker Crossen Big Band 25
Taxes (Musicians) 27, 28
Taylor, Jackie 56–58
Ten Commandments 110
Thaxton Brothers 97
Theresa Hotel 140
Thief's Journal 66
Thomas 11
Transgression Construct: Incarceration 94–96; Isolation 94, 96; Meditation 94, 96–99; Purification 94, 99–101; Challenge 95, 101, 102; Choice 95, 101, 102; Perfection 95, 102–105
Transgression of the Mind 13, 76, 77, 79, 83, 94, 95, 97, 98, 101, 102, 104, 105, 110, 120, 122, 129, 139, 142
Tremont Street 25
Trichinosis 87
Trumpet 7, 24, 25, 55
Tuscaroras 15

Uncle Toms 110
Union (Musician's) 25–28, 42
Union Baptist Church 16, 17, 21, 108
Union Secretary 26, 27
United States 12, 63, 109

Vaughn, Sarah 30
Victoria Hotel 46
Vietnam 21
Vodun 120
Voodoo 77
Voodoo Priest 75, 119

Wally's 26, 40, 42, 44, 49
Wang Center 26
War of 1812 (British and American) 15
Washington, D. C. 39, 109
Washington, Denzel 22, 137
Washington Park 39
Washington Street 26, 39, 56
Waumbec Street (#78) 33, 52
Webb, Chick 31
Webster's Unabridged Dictionary 88, 89

The West 118
West Coast 13
Western Society 118
White, Edna 17
White, Ethel Francis 15, 18
White, Etta 17
White, Eva 20, 21
White, Lou Virginia ("Aunt Jenny") 17
White, Lucy 17
White, Miles 17
White, Minerva 21
White, Peter Miles 16, 17
White, Priscilla ("Aunt Pree") 21
White, Roger 20, 21
White Girls 44, 45, 56, 63, 65

White Man 12, 60, 88–90, 107, 110–113, 120, 131
White Power Structure 109
White, Stella 21
Wilkins, Roy 144
Windsor Street 55
Winston Dictionary 111, 112
Witch Doctor 75, 119

Yates, Detective Harvey 49, 50
Yoruba High Priests 120
Young, Andrew 108

Zigfield Theater 23
Zoot Suits 33, 55

www.ingramcontent.com/pod-product-compliance
Ingram Content Group UK Ltd.
Pitfield, Milton Keynes, MK11 3LW, UK
UKHW042015140426
5217IPUK00015B/1192